Can of Worms
Real Answers to Relationship Issues

James Craig, PhD
&
Shawna Reinhardt

Zyntango Publishing
Books for Life Enrichment

Acknowledgements
Cover photo by Anne Heffernan
Editor Nancy Burrell

Like us on Facebook
https://www.facebook.com/CanOfWormsRelationships
/info

We would like to thank our families for their support and
contributions to our project.

Dedicated to Kiko Reinhardt – Angel in Heaven

Manufactured in the United States of America

Contents

About James Craig

About Shawna Reinhardt

Introduction/Instructions: Who is answering these questions and how can this book help me?

About James Craig

James Craig has more than 30 years of counseling education and practical experience. He earned a doctorate in professional counseling from Purdue University, as well as degrees in ministry and pastoral counseling from Lincoln Christian University and Seminary. He has served in community mental health, local church, and private practice settings. Dr. Craig is a Clinical Member of the American Association for Marriage and Family Therapy and a Licensed Marriage and Family Therapist. Jim and his wife Linda live in Indianapolis.

About Shawna Reinhardt

Shawna has spent the last 30+ years accumulating life experiences that make her uniquely qualified to write about the trials and tribulations of the modern relationship. She spent her formative years moving around the country with her parents, who were faced with challenges created by new locations, new jobs and not- so- marital bliss. Shawna completed a degree in management from Binghamton University and began a career that has been rewarding and full of challenges. As a wife and mother of three children, she is able to apply the content of this book to her life every day.

Purpose

This book demonstrates that Christian principles are relevant, whether articulated by an older marriage and family therapist with grown children, or a younger wife, mother, and entrepreneur raising young children. We hope readers of all ages find the authors' unique perspectives refreshing and helpful.

Introduction/Instructions

The book is arranged in question and answer format separated into sections by topic. The beginning of every topic will have an introduction. Along the way, discussion boxes will be indicated by a grey box.

Read them on your own, with your spouse or as part of a study group. This book may be read page by page, section by section, randomly or by looking for questions that grab your attention. We do encourage you though to read the whole book since a lot of the advice pertains to everyone.

We have left random whitespace for you to mark your thoughts along the way. If our questions inspire additional questions or thoughts, write them down for further discussion or thought.

This is not a running dialog. It provides answers from two life perspectives: One of a woman married for a few years with young children, and the other from a man married for decades with grown children. They won't always agree but will answer the questions in a way that is beneficial to all age groups.

Most of these questions came from hundreds of married couples attending marriage retreats, seminars, and workshops. At some point in the programs, Dr. Craig asked them to write provocative questions they might hesitate to ask publically—questions that revealed too much personal detail, or dealt with issues that would cause controversy and hurt feelings. The goal was to identify what was actually on these people's minds and hearts.

Others came from real-life interactions. Of course, we have changed all names and important identifying details to maintain confidentiality. However, we have retained the questions just as they were presented— no fluff, filler, or softened edges.

Chapter 1   The Myth of "Happily Ever After"

Have you ever noticed how our stories and romantic movies end with "and they lived happily ever after"? It's all about a proposal, wedding, baby, and a nice house in the suburbs. The myth begins for young women when our parents read us fairytales. Life is challenging for the young princess and then her prince comes to her rescue. They marry and live happily ever after. Who can really blame us for growing up and wanting our own 'happily ever after?' We are raised to expect it.

A prince may come sooner than later. Though he is not perfect, she thinks once they get married things will get better. Somehow putting a ring on her finger and spending oodles of money and time for a ceremony and reception will push the relationship to the next level of happiness.

Then it is time to buy a home together—the next big milestone event.   It consumes the couple's time and conversations. They buy the home and move in. Then comes all of the promising discussion about decorating, landscaping, furniture, appliances, window treatments and so on. As these are secured, and things begin to slow, the couple begins to realize that they don't have as much to discuss and don't really know each other as well as they thought. He leaves his dirty laundry all over the house, throws dirty dishes into the sink, and splatters so much toothpaste on the bathroom mirror that her reflection is distorted.

Oh but now she is pregnant! This is the BEST: more avoidance, more promises of a 'happily ever after'.

Now things are REALLY going to be great! He is going to be the most loving being and take care of her and the baby. She is going to be a kinder, gentler woman and not pick on him for his perpetually half-finished repair and remodeling projects. For a while, it is all about the baby.

The baby arrives and everyone is thrilled. They are surrounded by family and friends. As the weeks go by there are fewer helpers around. Life returns to normal. However, it isn't normal because they aren't getting more than a couple of hours of sleep at night. They haven't had time to be alone in months. They are tired, cranky and see laundry lying all over the bedroom. If this is 'happily ever after', they can keep it. This is not what they signed up for.

For some, the prince comes and the prince goes. Then another prince and another until she thinks there really aren't any princes out there. She becomes jaded and realizes the books and movies lied to her all those years. She may already own homes and cars. Careers and pets have become the substitute for a spouse and kids.

One day in her thirties or later, she wakes up and realizes she has done incredible things and had experiences others will never have, but she is kind of lonely. She has all sorts of friends and acquaintances, yet many of them are older and single as well. Then she meets someone special who has a similar history. They stop long enough to fall in love.

The couple watched friends get married in their early 20's, have children and then get divorced. They think, "That isn't going to happen to us, we are smarter than that." They see all of their friends' kids getting older and they feel left out. Ah, but wait, they are still smarter than those kids who ran off and got married in their 20's. They know that communication is very important and they have common life plans and goals.

Now they are married and want kids. The rush is on.

They have been trying for a year to have a baby but it isn't happening. Sex has become business. It is timed and planned. They are stressed and their marriage is strained. All they talk about now is having a baby. They finally get pregnant but are now considered higher risk and that too is very stressful. They wonder, "Where has the passion gone? How did we get to this point and how can we go back to a simpler time? We were so smart...how did we get to this point?"

They weren't going to be like all those other people who got married too early and didn't understand what life was really about. They had communication down pat but now can hardly communicate. They knew that marriage was a lot of work and are committed to make it work, but they need help. They ask, "what is wrong with us? Why isn't everything going the way we planned?"

In a third scenario, the couple has been married for 15 years. Their children are involved in a million activities. Husband/wife are busy ferrying the children around to all of their activities. Overall, they feel they have a pretty good family life. They eat dinner together a couple nights a week and go to the kids' sporting events on the weekends and church together as a family. However, they feel the interpersonal connection that makes marriage satisfying is lost.

Lastly, consider the empty nester. The children are getting ready to head off to college, the service, or a full time job. Now it is just two married people looking across the table thinking, "Who are you?" They have been so consumed by their children they don't even remember what it was like to be a couple. In some cases they have been staying together solely for the good of the children. Now what?

One more aspect to throw in is this: For those getting married at an older age, the spouse may bring baggage of an ex-spouse and/or stepchildren. This is an added complexity and strain on a relationship that is very common in today's world!

It doesn't really matter now how each couple got here. Here they are, in a relationship that is not exactly what they dreamed it would be.   This is the problem with "And they lived happily ever after." The fairy tale endings of movies are the endings!. If they continued, we would see that fairy tales dissolve into real life issues. Notice that "Cinderella 2" or "Sleepless in Seattle: The Sequel" have not been made!

We need to push these unrealistic expectations from our minds and realize that life throws a lot of monkey wrenches into our plans. As soon as we have it all planned out, it inevitably changes. We cannot control every aspect of life. We need to give the control to God and realize we can and should plan but we also need to be open to changes and opportunities that come along the way. If we are always trying to get to the 'happily ever after' ending, we will miss the happiness along the way.

Chapter 2   Sexual Intimacy

Question 1: **Why do men think sex makes everything O.K?**

Question 2: **How do I get my husband to initiate sex?**

Question 3: **What is a male idea of a romantic evening?**

Question 4: **What are the scriptural issues dealing with vasectomy and other permanent birth control methods?**

Question 5: **Any ideas to help a husband be more verbal during foreplay?**

Question 6: **Why is sex so important to a husband?**

Question 7: **What do you do about not being interested in sex?**

Question 8: **How can you bring "real" feelings, passion, and romance back to your marriage when it has grown VERY COLD?**

Question 9: **What can you do when there is no passion for God, love, work, sex, etc. in your marriage?**

Question 10: **How can we be romantic when children are around?**

Question 11: **How do you deal with the physical weakness of growing old?**

Question 12: **How far does a couple go in trying to please each other? Should one go ahead and do things that he/she normally would not want to do just to please the spouse?**

Question 13: **Is sex the same thing as intimacy?**

Question 14: **We are not proud of it, but we did have sex before marriage. How can we get back the excitement we felt then?**

Question 15: **How does one truly "leave and cleave" when family members will be hurt and the spouse is terrified of being rejected by the family?**

Sexual Intimacy

Like it or not, questions about sexual intimacy are the first questions asked in the retreat setting. Often, couples attend retreats to settle arguments about sex and its meaning in their marriage. This is why we decided to answer these questions first.

It is common for Christian married couples to report having a happier, more secure sex life than their secular counterparts. Sex and security have always been partners, and nothing provides security like Christ-centered faithfulness in a context of honesty and mutual submission.

Even so, when given the opportunity, most Christian couples express significant frustration with this aspect of relationship. They are reluctant to talk to their pastors about these issues, especially in those church traditions where discussion of sexuality is considered off-limits. They often talk with family/friends about this aspect of their lives as well as being influenced by modern day culture.

Question 1: Why do men think sex makes everything O.K.?

Young brides and older wives alike ask this question. Both complain their husbands are tender only when they want to make love. Both may withhold affection to prove the point, "When you can touch me without expecting sex, then I will be attracted to you."

A wife who rejects her husband on this point puts him in an impossible position. If he corrects his faults under such pressure, he confirms her suspicions. If he refuses to correct his faults, he confirms her suspicions. This is a hopeless situation guaranteed to foster anger and chaos.

God forbids such no-win games. Biblically speaking, the woman who punishes her husband by withholding sex disobeys God, exposes herself and her spouse to sexual temptation, and denies herself the pleasure God intended in the marital relationship (see I Corinthians 7:5).

No-win sex games begin at both ends of the ideological spectrum. For example, some women raised in ultra-conservative religious traditions believe sex is nothing more than a necessary evil to propagate the human race. Ironically, their attitudes and behavior closely resemble those of the most radical feminists who might believe that heterosexual intercourse is nothing more than legalized rape. Both are likely to feel injured and dirty after intercourse, ashamed of their physical desires, and deeply offended by their mates' enjoyment. They are also likely to see the pain of childbearing as confirmation of their beliefs and good reason to avoid future contact. These ideas promote chronic sexual frustration, explosive arguments, dissatisfaction, and the alienation of fathers and their children.

Some men really do believe that sex renders all other matters unimportant. They seek vulnerable women who have a history of trading sex for empty promises. Wedding licenses and parroted vows cannot correct this fundamental character flaw. Neither can more empty promises, like, "I'll try to cut down on my drinking" nor "I promise I'll never cheat again."

In sound, committed marriages, sex does make some things OK. God has created it for our mutual benefit and enjoyment. In obedience to Him, married couples should:

➤ Consider regular, satisfying sexual relations as essential to the health of their marriage.
➤ Insist on developing other intimacy *in addition to* sexual intimacy rather than *as a condition for* sexual intimacy.

It is hard for a woman to answer this question without seeming rude to men. My guess is that some men think if their wife is willing to have sex then things must be fine. Also, most men usually feel better after they have sex…so why wouldn't they think things were fine?

Question 2: How do I get my husband to initiate sex?

I am thinking about a couple with whom I worked recently. The wife complained bitterly that her husband is completely unromantic and insensitive. "I've told him what I want, but he doesn't care about my feelings!" she charged. He virtually exploded. "You're never satisfied! You say you want flowers, but when I give you flowers, you scream that they aren't roses!"

Their marriage had degenerated into a grand failed love test—"If you really loved me, you would know my needs" and "If you really loved me, you would be satisfied."

It is wrong to test a mate in this manner. It is also wrong to irk a mate by intentionally failing tests. Someone has to break this stalemate, and it is usually the one who is more spiritually mature.

Some men are shy and need to be coaxed. Others believe they have tried to initiate, been rejected, and decided not to try again. In either case, a wife who wants to improve the situation can:

➤ Ask her husband honestly "Is there something I do or have done that prevents you from initiating lovemaking?"
➤ Give him time to respond, avoiding the temptation to defend, interrupt, or argue.
➤ Abandon Hollywood standards for romance.
➤ Participate willingly when he initiates.
➤ Be patient.
➤ Never criticize him for being shy, awkward or uncertain.

As Jim mentioned, when your husband does initiate, respond positively. If you respond in a negative way because you are tired or busy with something else, he may give up and stop trying. If you are too tired or not feeling right when he initiates, give him a sense of hope by letting him know that you appreciate it and you would love to reconvene at a later time.

Be conscientious of the fact that men have feelings too. Your husband may be having some sort of issue that he is self- conscious about. Maybe the last couple of times you had sex it didn't live up to your standards and it made him feel inadequate. He may feel that he can't please you or live up to the expectation so it is easier to not try at all. As Jim says, don't criticize him. When sex is over, don't complain if the time was too short or he was in the wrong position. If he is already self- conscious it will not likely encourage him to initiate in the future.

Does he respond when you initiate? If so, you should initiate a few times and reassure him when you are finished that you enjoyed being with him.

Question 3: What is a male idea of a romantic evening?

Contrary to modern myth, men are not push-button performers. We enjoy being lavished with loving attention and thoughtful companionship, too. For a guy-style romantic evening, a couple can: Hire a baby sitter and put everyday worries on hold for the evening, go to an action movie, a sporting goods store, a jazz club, or some other place the husband likes, stop for a snack and a long cup of coffee on the way home, and lock the bedroom door.

Many women would assume the short answer to this question would be food and sex. I decided to poll a few of my under 40 male friends:

> Babysitter
> Dressed for location/environment
> Special location
> Special Lighting
> Good Food
> End the evening with sex

Question 4: What are the scriptural issues dealing with vasectomy and other permanent birth control methods?

The scriptural issues surrounding this topic include (but are not limited to) the responsibilities for procreation, being a submissive helpmate, enjoying sexual intimacy, care for the unborn, and understanding of the dangers of bringing children into a dangerous world. Having taken these and other scriptural issues into account, I have concluded that Christian couples may use permanent birth control measures which do not cause abortion. To study this thoroughly, couples can:

➢ Sit down and write down their initial thoughts about this issue.
➢ Use an exhaustive Bible concordance to find all references to birth and children.
➢ Go to a Christian bookstore that sells pro-life materials and select a few books that deal with these ethical issues.
➢ Consult competent pro-life pastors and physicians for guidance.

On a personal note, my husband and I recently had our second baby and I have a stepdaughter as well. We are still discussing this issue for ourselves and our family. I am ambivalent on this question. A lot of ladies in my position are thinking of having more children but are aware of the physical dangers and the financial cost and trying to exercise responsible stewardship in their lives.

Question 5: Any ideas to help a husband be more verbal during foreplay?

A woman can be starved for words of love and tenderness. She can start making things better by sharing this concern with her husband and defining it as her need rather than his inadequacy. It is helpful to for her to:

➤ Admit that she was initially attracted to his strength and silence.
➤ Guard against demanding too much too quickly and becoming chronically disappointed.
➤ Be patient as he learns to open up.

I read this question and thought it may not only be women who feel this way but men as well. Neither gender wants to feel judged or rated in the bedroom. Yet often times the other person is secretly wishing for feedback or new ideas and suggestions but both parties may be too afraid to bring up the topic.

The key here is to gently suggest to your spouse in a non-accusatory way that it may heat things up if he/she expressed certain things to you during foreplay. When your spouse starts expressing, it is your obligation to respond and not laugh or ridicule him/her for what they say. The key here is to respond in a positive way.

Question 6: Why is sex so important to a husband?

A stand-up comedian came dangerously close to the truth when he said, "Men will do anything for sex, even love a woman. Women will do anything for love, even have sex with a man."
The facts of life include:

➤ For men, sex provides a sense of excitement, mystery, competence, dominance, submission, achievement, warmth, love, being needed, wanted, and successful. This presents both opportunity (for procreation and intimacy) and temptation (for fornication, adultery, and idolatry).
➤ Men reach their "prime" in terms of sexual desire at age 16 and decline slowly as they get older.
➤ Women experience an increase in interest until they reach their "prime" around age 35.
➤ Couples should be patient with each other, looking forward to the day when their desires will be fairly equal.

While there is certainly physical enjoyment involved, husbands just like wives benefit from the emotional connection they feel from being intimate.   The lack of sex can mean a lot to a man such as a sense of rejection and inadequacy.

Question 7: What do you do about not being interested in sex?

A person suffering the lack of sexual desire can also ask, "What prevents me from being more interested in sex?" With some soul searching, a spouse may discover one of several problems including simple exhaustion or anemia; a deep feeling of being unattractive, unlovely or unlovable; and/or a false religious belief that sex is dirty. Also, lack of sexual interest often indicates anger surrounding broken trust—a consequence of both real and imagined violations. Couples can address the diminished desire by:

➢ Resting up and receiving the medical care, nutrition, and exercise they need.
➢ Dressing up, making the most of their most attractive features.
➢ Reading and following what the Bible actually says about sex.
➢ Listening to what mature Christian authorities say.
➢ Confessing sin, offering and accepting Christ's forgiveness.

Relax. Stress, lack of sleep, not taking care of yourself all take a toll on you and can decrease your desire for sex. Sometimes you just need to initiate it! It doesn't always have to be hours of foreplay and candles. Sometimes you should just go do it, enjoy it for the calories you will burn and the stress you will release. Chemicals are released during sex that are beneficial to you and your stress levels. Additionally, it will benefit your partner and your marriage. From a female perspective, it is sometimes true that the more often you have sex with your spouse the more often you will want to have sex with your spouse. The longer you go without it the less you may tend to think about it and fall into a rut of not having it.

For women, a large part of wanting to have sex starts with an emotional state. If a woman does not feel emotionally connected to her husband, it may be more challenging for her to feel interested in sex. If this is the case, you need to speak with your partner and possibly a counselor about ways the two of you can work on reconnecting.

You may be bored with sex or it isn't enjoyable for you. Talk with your partner about this. You may benefit from speaking with a counselor.

There could be another issue here as well. If your partner had an issue performing at one time or another, it could have caused an uncomfortable situation for both of you. If that is the case, there are tactful ways to let your spouse know there have been studies showing that it might be linked to other health related issues. He or she should be encouraged to see their doctor and have a full physical.

Please refer back to the earlier answer regarding hygiene. If your partner has poor hygiene habits, it may be a severe turn off for you.

Question 8: How can you bring "real" feelings, passion, and romance back to your marriage when it has grown VERY COLD?

A woman who believes her husband is exceptionally distracted, disinterested, and thoughtless might ask this. A man who is concerned about his wife's lack of sexual desire and/or responsiveness will express similar concerns.

At times, the root of the problem lies in the poisoned soil of pornography. Men watch filmy undulating images and read dirty magazines, while women flock to "chick flicks" and immerse themselves in steamy romance novels. Both develop a view of sex that is completely self-serving and impossibly unrealistic.

True love does not happen spontaneously, but is cultivated by two people who care about meeting each other's needs with patience and passion. Sadly, some married couples will never openly discuss or deal with these issues. They are content to escape into their individual fantasies, blaming the other for failure to make them come true. They use work, family, and church obligations to avoid intimacy.

Thankfully, the salvation of Jesus Christ is a comprehensive salvation, touching every aspect of life. To access the benefits of this saving grace, it is important to:

➢ Stop blaming.
➢ Start forgiving.
➢ Trust that God will restore intimacy.

18

This is a very serious issue that can lead to cheating. It might seem that your relationship is so distant that reconnecting is not likely. Cheating is messy, hurtful to everyone and the effects long lasting.

To reengage and reenergize your marriage:

➢ Start with having an open mind and heart.
➢ Try talking with your spouse about wanting to reengage and energize your relationship.
➢ Reassure your spouse that it isn't a time for blame. Rather it is an opportunity to experience a positive and uplifting time as you reengage one another on a deeper level than the first time you dated.
➢ Work on the exercises together found throughout this book.
➢ Pretend you know nothing about each other and court one another, just as you did when you met.
➢ Make an effort and do things that may seem silly to you now but wouldn't seem silly to two people dating.
➢ If you cannot break through the communication barrier that has built up, seek out a family counselor who can help get you started. Let the counselor know that you want to rediscover one another and rebuild your relationship but need help getting started.

Exercise: Be Nice!

Try this exercise for 30 days: Make a conscious effort to do or say something nice/complimentary to one another. Don't do it because you expect something in return. It doesn't need to be something that takes a lot of time or costs money. Simple gestures are often the most meaningful and endearing. If you are both working on this together, be sure to accept the compliments and appreciate your spouse's effort and sincerity.

Question 9: What can you do when there is no passion for God, love, work, sex, etc. in your marriage?

"No passion" is a physical, emotional, relational, and spiritual problem. It can be caused by the use of alcohol, illegal drugs, prescription medications, poor diet, lack of exercise, unresolved anger, chronic disappointment, pessimism, and lack of purpose. Good physicians and pastors can help couples:

➢ Stop drinking, smoking, over-medicating, eating junk food, and/or sitting in front of the TV for entertainment.
➢ Find their place in the Body of Christ, encouraging them to use their gifts and abilities in effective ministry as well as allowing others to minister to them.

A lack of passion is often the result of depression, failure, or fear of rejection. Talk with a trusted advisor from your church or a counselor to help identify what the issues might be. Something simple like getting more sleep or exercising a few times a week might be the answer for you.

Turn off the electronic devices including TV, video games, computers and phones. No, not all the time, we often need to be reachable for our kids, parents etc. However, make an effort to prioritize time for the important things.

Question 10: How can we be romantic when children are around?

Being romantic includes many behaviors, including (but not limited to) buying personal gifts for each other, turning off the TV and talking, and going out. A child needs to know his/her parents are attracted to each other and that they expect him to be attracted to his/her spouse someday too. Parents can do this by:

➤ Modestly and discretely, showing their children how much they love each other.
➤ When the kids scream, "Yuck!", and giggle, parents can laugh and tell them they will feel the same way someday.
➤ Going out together, preferring each other's company, and locking the bedroom door. These actions increase the romance quotient while silently affirming sex as a mysterious, private, wonderful relationship from which children are excluded.

Holding hands, kissing and hugging can and should all be done with children around. When the children take a nap, go to school or to bed, you can be more romantic...

Question 11: How do you deal with the physical weakness of growing old?

Questions like this can reflect a concern with sexual performance. The word "performance" is the key, and often the main problem. If marital sex is a "performance", partners become athletes who grow frustrated as raw ability diminishes with age. To escape the performance trap, couples can:

➢ Discuss their general and sexual health with a physician, understanding that drugs (e.g. blood pressure and mood-altering medications) and other physical infirmities can diminish the libido.
➢ Practice good personal hygiene, understanding that a potbelly, bad breath, untrimmed nose and ear hair, and body odor can passively express contempt for one's spouse.
➢ Discuss differing views of marital sex with a Christian pastor and/or marriage counselor.

There are also items that can assist with the physical aspect of this question. For example, positioners, cushions, wedges, etc., can make a couple more comfortable and help alleviate weakness or pain from arthritis.

Those who have an on-going problem with ED (Erectile Dysfunction) would do well to visit a doctor for a physical. ED issues may possibly be a sign of something more serious related to heart health, diabetes, cholesterol, etc. Having an issue every now and again isn't an issue. We all have our "off times" and really should not be taken too seriously unless it is frequent. However, if it becomes a big deal it can become a mental block for future attempts.

When I read Jim's answer about practicing good personal hygiene I laughed to myself and thought this applies across all ages and is not limited to growing older. If you drink alcohol, smoke, chew tobacco, eat garlic, or drink a lot of coffee, you should be aware that it may be leaving your mouth less than desirable for your spouse.

Question 12: How far does a couple go in trying to please each other? Should one go ahead and do things that he/she normally would not want to do just to please the spouse?

In addition to God-given physiological and psychological differences, men and women bring a variety of expectations to the marital bed. With the exceptions of sodomy (anal intercourse), masturbation used as substitute for sexual intercourse, and physical cruelty, the Bible does not seem to limit what a husband and wife choose to do sexually. Instead, the Bible commands absolute fidelity, urges sexual joy, provides general relational precepts, and specifically charges husbands to lead by loving in a sacrificial manner.

Husbands often desire a more adventurous sex life. Wives, too, can become bored with the 'same old same old'. However, often the husband desires a wilder relationship while the wife longs for more tenderness, security, and romance. If a husband wants sexual relations with his wife in a context of mutual love and tenderness, his expectation is biblically justified. A wife who consistently refuses is disobeying God, hurting her marriage, and exposing herself and her mate to temptation. However, if the husband expects oral sex, freedom to indulge in wild fantasies, and/or the use of sex toys, the wife's conscience may truly be violated.

Sadly, to some men, "good sex" is that which is seen in pornographic literature and films. Likewise, some women want the so-sensitive hunk featured in the latest romance novel or movie. Both will be disappointed. Those who want the real thing should:

25

➢ Understand that many of today's sexual ideals are lies fabricated by people who hate God and which are communicated through powerful entertainment media and cultural myth.

➢ Read the Proverbs and Song of Solomon for some very graphic descriptions of marital love within the holiness of God's Word.

➢ Consult their pastor and/or Christian marriage counselor to confess sin, receive forgiveness, and establish realistic expectations.

You should never do something just to please someone else. My grandmother used to say if you are going to do something do it with joy in your heart. Be sincere about it!. Adding some adventure to the bedroom to spice things up every now and then is not necessarily a bad thing and can add a new element to your bedroom life.

My personal thought on this is to be open-minded about what your spouse would like to try as long as it is not humiliating or hurtful. If it doesn't offend you morally and you are comfortable trying it, then you should. Let your spouse know you will try it once and have an open mind. Agree ahead of time that if you don't like it you will not be badgered about it again.

Dialogue: Your Desires

After several years of a loving marriage and a couple of children, Julia had an affair with her personal trainer. She called her friends to tell them about the best sex she had ever had in her life. Julia loved her husband but he was so boring in the bedroom that she had lost all interest in him. He was so routine that it was the exact same five minutes every time. She would try and encourage different positions or a new room in the house but he was pretty stuck in his ways. Julia wasn't in love with her trainer but was so torn about her marriage; she loved her husband's company but she couldn't find it in herself to be with him physically anymore. They wound up divorced, miserable and both alone.

The moral of this sad but true story is that relationships aren't like TV/magazines/movies. All relationships take effort and this is true in the bedroom as well. If it becomes dry and routine with the exact same moves for years, I am sure you can see where that got Julia and her husband.

Set a time in the near future when you can talk specifically about your desires and the possibilities of adding variety to your life. If this is a sore topic, it might be a good to do this in the presence of a marriage counselor.

Question 13: Is sex the same thing as intimacy?

Sex is not intimacy. It is one kind of intimacy. Sadly, sex is often used as a substitute for both marital intimacy and true sexual intimacy.

Marital intimacy includes friendship, community, ministry, a sense of wonder, the sharing of joys and sorrows, caring for each other, working together for the common good, brotherhood, fellowship, and benevolence. True sexual intimacy is a subset of marital intimacy, a physical pleasure enjoyed within an edifying context of security and commitment.

An healthy couple enjoys both sexual and non-sexual intimacy. Couples who want to enhance their intimacy can:

➤ Think of intimacy as a series of bridges.
➤ Think of sex as a wonderful, delicate bridge which will not be able to bear the heavier burdens of the relationship.
➤ Build other bridges that are more substantial.

Sex is one kind of intimacy, but it isn't the only or most important kind. You can have great intimacy without ever having sex. There are couples with physical challenges who cannot have a sexual relationship but are still able to have great intimacy with one another without the physical act of sex.

This form of intimacy is one reason that it is important to avoid chat rooms, social networking sites and other opportunities for online intimacy with the opposite sex. This can lead to a form of intimacy which equals cheating on your spouse even if you have never met the other person.

28

Exercise: The Meaning of Sex
Once you and your spouse have identified these answers individually, discuss them together. Remember, the way sex is glorified in books, movies and TV is not reality.

➤ Ask yourself, What does sex mean to you?
➤ What do you want to get out of it?
➤ Is it intimacy?
➤ Are you hoping for an emotional connection?
➤ Are you hoping to feel closer to your spouse?
➤ Do you want to just have fun with your spouse?
➤ Does your desire/frequency vary based on monthly hormone cycles?

Question 14: We are not proud of it, but we did have sex before marriage. How can we get back the excitement we felt then?

It is impossible to get back to a previous level of excitement for two reasons. First, time has worn the newness off the sexual relationship. Second, marriage has eliminated the sweet taste of forbidden fruit. Perhaps the only way to "get back" to the old days is to cheat on each other—an exceedingly foolish thing to do!

Unmarried Christian couples often counsel with pastors to confess having premarital sex. They ask, "How can we stop doing this until we are married?" Pastors can help by leading a couple to discuss their spiritual beliefs, vision for the future, money, kids, friends, and in-laws. They need to know they have been using sex to avoid deeper intimacy.

As mentioned above, intimacy can be thought of as a series of bridges.   These must be carefully built and religiously maintained. Sex is a fun yet fragile bridge. It simply will not bear the weight of life difficulties, as any couple with a baby suffering an inner ear infection can testify!

Biblical love is the most difficult bridge to build, but it is the only one that will carry the load when others collapse. To repair their sexual bridge, couples can:

➤ Develop true intimacy by attending church together, taking long walks, sharing their faith, and discussing their hopes and dreams.
➤ Consult a Christian counselor and ask for help in becoming more intimate.

The excitement experienced when a relationship is new is fleeting and temporary. It can be conjured by TV, society, and the advice of friends. In the beginning, uncertainty enhanced excitement. Once a couple is married, both people know they can have sex with each other anytime. From a female perspective, the anticipation of becoming engaged and married can also stimulate a sense of excitement. Before marriage, there were no mortgage payments or kids keeping you awake all night.

It is still important to be spontaneous. If a couple always has sex at the same time twice a week and on holidays it will become too routine. Sex doesn't have to be an improv performance every time, but it shouldn't always be scripted either.

Question 15: How does one truly "leave and cleave" when family members will be hurt and the spouse is terrified of being rejected by the family?

Leaving one's parents and cleaving to one's spouse is an act of godly will and courage. Good parents want their children to leave, spend years preparing them to go, look forward to the freedom of the empty nest, and have no intention of inviting them back for more than a temporary visit.

My mother-in-law delivered a sobering message one sultry July afternoon in 1974. Returning from our honeymoon, Linda and I decided to stop at her parents' house to pick up some of our wedding gifts. Her mother answered the door and said "I hope you aren't planning to stay for dinner—we have two guests coming and only four pork chops." (I am no rocket scientist, but I can do the math on that one!)

My parents feel the same way. Just a few years ago, I came home from work and noticed the answering machine was flashing "one message". It was my mom. She had called to let us know they had headed for Florida to visit her sister, did not know where they would be staying, and did not know when they would be back. In other words, she was saying, "We have a life apart from you. Don't call us, we'll call you!"

If a family rejects its married children for doing what God has called them to do, then the motive is selfishness, not love. Christ constantly addressed this problem, *even teaching his disciples to disown their families if necessary*. (This teaching was not addressed to parents, but to children whose Jewish parents forbade them to follow Him.) The following guidelines are timeless. Good kids will always:

- ➢ Honor their parents by doing the good things they have taught them to do and thanking them for their guidance.
- ➢ Leave and cleave.
- ➢ Understand that if parents have problems with this arrangement, they really have problems with God's Word.

If you are old enough to be married you are old enough to leave your parents. That doesn't mean that you can't spend time with them. It is natural for kids to want to go off and discover their own way when they become teens. It is hard for parents to accept but this part of the maturation process preparing them to become adults. I don't understand parents who let their 30-something `kids' move in with them and never leave. They are not teaching their children how to survive. Don't misunderstand, there are times to help your family out but not without a plan for how to get the kids back on their own two feet.

Marriage means making a commitment. Remember "who gives this woman..."? That person/s GAVE you to this man. Now you have a mate with whom you should be sharing everything. Decisions are between the two of you. You can still ask others for advice but the two of you need to evaluate all the options and advice and make decisions together.

This is probably more your parents issue than yours. Some parents just can't let go because they live their lives through their children. They need to get back into the world and make their own friendship connections and volunteer, etc. Guilt trips are hurtful. Just remember how it feels so that you can break the cycle with your own children.

Furthermore, your spouse should not be worried that your family won't like him if he has integrity and treats you and your children the right way. My guess is that he is afraid he will lose you if your family doesn't like him. We have already established that parents are the ones who need to let go and let you be the adult you are.

D ialogue: Men Behaving Intimately on the Internet

Where can men go for reliable guidance concerning "intimacy"? According to politicians and educators, we must turn to the Internet! Following their lead, I logged-on, searched for the words "intimacy and men", and found lots of stuff, most of which cannot be described in good taste. Among the so-called "legitimate" sites were:

➢ New Age counseling centers which help men "reach for the supportive, vital world they envision and reclaim the ability to think and decide in ways true to themselves":
➢ Personal web pages devoted to men whose wives are not as interested in sex as they are
➢ Ads for schools which teach Eastern religious cleansing rites for the menstruating woman; and
➢ Businesses specializing in men's physique photography.

In addition to pornography and New Age nonsense, the Internet offers men an illusion of intimacy—an opportunity to "chat" with who-knows-what and pretend to have a close, personal relationship. Counselors are seeing more and more people who report being hooked on and victimized by these phony friendships.

Dialogue Starters:
➢ What is the difference between an illusion of intimacy and real intimacy?
➢ Besides sexual intimacy, what kind of intimacy can a husband and wife share?
➢ In what ways does the local church tend to help or hinder such intimacy?

Chapter 3　　　Children

Question 1: **God commands that we serve Him, and He has also blessed us with children. Should a person "forsake" his family to serve God?**

Question 2: **How do you stop a stepson from pitting parents and stepparents against each other?**

Question 3: **How is it possible to love a stepchild as your own?**

Question 4: **How can I enforce Christian principles (regarding movies, school dances, etc.) in my pre-teen without making him feel like a geek with his friends?**

Question 5: **My mom never let me do chores because I never could do them to suit her. My kids are teenagers and I have done the same to them. Is it too late to teach them responsibility?**

Question 6: **How can a wife be supportive when she disagrees with the way her husband disciplines the children? (Discussion always leads to anger and fights, and nothing gets resolved.)**

Question 7: **I am lucky to be a stay-at-home mom. Why do I feel so discouraged?**

Question 8: **My husband has been offered a promotion, but it means a move. Should we do this to our children?**

Question 9: **My parents have offered to buy a car for our 16-year-old son. Should we let them do this?**

Question 10: **With an 8 month old, I feel like my husband and I are further apart than before our child was born. How do you suggest we get a closer relationship?**

Question 11: **Everything has become about the children, even with our friends. What about us?**

Question 12: **How can we teach our children to avoid the pitfalls we have experienced?**

Question 13: **When is 'grown-up' honesty too much for children? For example, my spouse is a recovering addict. At what age should we explain this to our children?**

Question 14: **Should we talk to and/or involve our children in our marriage counseling?**

Question 15: **My spouse and I have been fighting. Our son has always been a model child. Now we are getting calls from school about his poor behavior. I believe he is responding to the tension in our home. What should we do?**

Question 16: **My ex and I have three teenage children. They are asking me why we broke up. What can I share that will help them learn from our experience? My ex is still very bitter about our separation.**

Question 17: **My husband's ex-wife provokes conflict between my husband and me. For example, she changes schedules at the last minute and it creates chaos for our family. We end up fighting. Why does he take his anger out on me?**

Question 18: **My husband pushes our children to excel in sports. Our son is a very gifted musician and doesn't have much interest in sports but plays to please my husband.   How can I get through to my husband that not everyone needs to participate in sports?**

Question 19: **My spouse and I are empty nesters. The holidays are around the corner and our daughter is going on vacation with her friends. Should I confront her about this and tell her how upset her dad and I are that she is not coming home?**

Question 20: **My parents are divorced and both remarried. They are amicable, yet I still notice some jealousy, especially related to their time with the grandkids. We don't mean to favor either set of grandparents. How do we handle this?**

Question 21: **My husband pays support, alimony and other expenses of his ex-wife.   However, when the ex sends the kids to our house for new sports equipment, school supplies, shoes, coats etc., he obliges. We are struggling to pay our own bills and afford similar items for our other children. He lets her manipulate him which leads to arguments between us. Why can't he say no and stand up for our family?**

Children

Talk about risky behavior! Bearing and raising children are among the most difficult things humans can do. Good parenting takes courage, perseverance, and wisdom. Thankfully, God's Word is a rich source of all three.

As a marriage and family therapist, I often work with troubled young people and their frustrated parents. Kids rebel. Parents provoke. Kids play parents against each other. One parent joins the kids against the other parent. Grandparents join the kids against parents. Stepparents, extended family members, teachers, and pastors get involved. The unhappy possibilities are endless. The only hope for parents is to secure and practice God's principles for rearing healthy children.

Question 1: God commands that we serve Him, and He has also blessed us with children. Should a person "forsake" his family to serve God?

Consider the man or woman who becomes inordinately involved in the activities of the church. He attends every service, volunteers for every committee, is always the first one to sign up for various programs, spends every free moment working at church, and recruits others to do the same. She is in the nursery every time the building is open, substitutes for any Sunday school teacher who fails to show up, volunteers to keep the visiting missionaries in her home, produces the bulletins, plays piano for the choir, launders the baptismal robes, orders communion supplies, and organizes the Vacation Bible School program every year.

Both have held every elected office the church offers, and when the current officials drop the ball, they always jump in to finish the task. Both are the first ones other church leaders call when a job needs to be done yesterday. Both are married and have children. Both have spouses who are lonely and resentful of the church and its endless demands. Both have kids who are justifiably sick of standing around the church lobby waiting for dad or mom to take them home.

Ask them why they are so immersed in church life, and they will smile and politely deny that they do all that much. Dig a little deeper, and you will find they are using church work to avoid troubling marriage, family, and personal problems.

Neglect is not the answer, nor is cloning. The answer is making marriage, family, and church involvement an *integrated first priority*. The following are the strategies of parents who are succeeding in this endeavor. Wise parents:

- Worship Christ, not kids. They do not feel religiously obligated to attend every game or concert, nor do they live their lives through their children.
- Understand the difference between church work and the work of the Church. They do not feel religiously obligated to attend every service, meeting, social get-together, or ceremony.
- Respectfully excuse themselves from church meetings and programs which impede their ability to shepherd their family. They are not afraid to say "I promised I would be home by 8 tonight. Please excuse me."
- Make themselves accountable to church leaders. Regularly, in word and deed, they ask a trusted pastor or elder "Honestly, from your vantage point, am I using 'family' to shirk my ministry responsibilities?" and "How can I be more effective in both areas?"
- Plan and lead programs that strengthen families. Rather than abdicating leadership to others and complaining, they pro-actively participate in planning and implementing family-friendly programming.

NO, you should not forsake your family in the name of "God". I know the order is God, Family, and Work but that doesn't mean that ALL of your time goes to God things. Ideally, you should be able to do things that serve God and involve your family. A good example is how you live your life, are you living it for you or for God? You may be helping at church because you like the recognition and status. This is not better than being at home reading or spending time with your family.

Question 2: How do you stop a stepson from pitting parents and stepparents against each other?

Well-meaning teachers and counselors often say, "Your parents' divorce was not your fault. It had nothing to do with you." Such statements betray humanistic naiveté. While children do not cause divorce, they certainly do exacerbate and exploit parental conflict. Emotionally separated parents are easy prey. Physically separated, divorced, and remarried parents are even easier prey!

Teenagers are especially good at driving wedges between authority figures. Securing maximum freedom with minimum responsibility is their goal. We have evidence that this is true across cultures. Provoking parents, stepparents, teachers, etc. to blame each other is a universal method of teenagers. Chaos is always the result.

Left uncorrected, such behavior leads to a life of trouble. This is the central meaning of the Fifth Commandment. Honor for parents and cultural continuity go hand in hand.

In a sense, the rebellious young person is asking, "Does anyone care enough about me to keep me from destroying myself?" Fragmented parents answer "No", wring their hands, and watch the wreck. Unified parents shout "Yes!" and begin building the necessary fences and retaining walls.

Wise parents have specific, pro-active strategies to keep their kids from playing them off against each other. For example, they:

> Seal the cracks. Wise parents don't pretend their children can't see their marital problems. They assume the children see them and exploit them

intentionally. If you are unable to agree on rules, consequences, and follow-through, it is likely that you have fundamental differences that must be settled. Close the bedroom door, argue quietly, and come out unified. If you cannot do this on your own, seek the help of a pastor or a counselor. Kids can be corralled if the parents will take the time to seal the cracks.

➢ Lose the hammer. Stop using the kids to hurt your ex-spouse. When parents divorce, they usually have a great deal of leftover anger and bitterness. They may verbally complain that the kids are misbehaving, but tacitly be happy because it "proves" the ex-spouse is to blame for the family problems. Comments like "Sure, Johnny is drinking! What do you expect from a son of yours?" and "Of course Sally ran away with her boyfriend! She's just like her slut-mother!" betray a selfish willingness to use a child's problems to justify one's own hatred.

➢ Let others help. Though they be imperfect, your church, Bible school class, and small group offer the support and encouragement of others who are facing or have faced similar challenges. Stop the "Yes, but . . . " routine and start listening to what your preachers, teachers, and friends are saying.

➢ Trust God's promises. In the long run, kids act pretty much as they are expected to act. If you secretly believe they are hopeless, you will give up prematurely and they will prove you right. If you believe God will bless your efforts, you will persevere and they will prove you right.

Teenagers in general tend to push the boundaries as they are becoming more independent.   Even if parents remain married in a healthy relationship, they would experience normal teenage antics. It doesn't mean teenagers are bad children or that they hate the parents, so try to not take it too personally. Having the divorce issue does add some complexity since you are not the only disciplinarians.

Parents need to sit down with the stepson and let him know that this behavior will not be tolerated on either side. He is loved by all but he needs to respect all parents. They should also make him aware that they share EVERYTHING with each other. Then the stepparent and parent need to do just that - share everything.

The son could be acting out because he doesn't know how to communicate how he feels about his parents' divorce. He may need family counseling to help express how he is feeling.

Question 3: How is it possible to love a stepchild as your own?

Christ-centered love is not an emotion, but a commitment. Honest parents and stepparents admit that they feel differently about each of their children. They work to listen to each child, identify each one's needs, and move to meet those needs individually. I recommend that parents:

➢ Start with candor. Admit to your spouse and children "I feel differently about each of you. Sometimes I let my emotions cloud my judgment. But by God's power, I promise to love each of you and do what is best for you."
➢ Finish with follow-through, providing love and discipline tailored to each child's needs.
➢ Illustrate your resolve by purchasing a creative, surprise gift for each child reflecting his/her taste or personality. For example, a father of three might come home some evening with three T-shirts, each with the name of that child's favorite college or pro team. If all three kids like the same team, the father might select different colors or designs to reflect the differences in their temperament. Even if the kids don't like the T-shirts, they will get the message—"Dad loves all of us, but recognizes the clear differences between us."

Children are a gift from God. When you marry their parent, the children become a part of your family. Unconditional love is part of being a family. It is important to keep in mind that children have external influences that affect their behavior and you don't have control over that. Try to think of them

45

as your children yet respect that you aren't their replacement mom or dad. Keep in mind that it is hard for them as well to go back and forth between homes and not to have both of their parents around all the time. If the other parent is saying bad things about your home, there is even more reason to take the high road. Rise above it and be the best parent and role model you can for that child.

If you have your own children, think of how you would want them to be treated if they had stepparents. How you treat all your children is what you are teaching your children. If a stepchild senses love and respect from you and doesn't feel like a third wheel at your house, it will help all of you bond and grow the relationship.

We are careful to call our house "home". We make the children feel special that they get to have two homes! This is just as much their home as it is their siblings who live here full-time. We also don't use the words "half-sister" or "half-brother". They are sisters and brothers, period!

Question 4: How can I enforce Christian principles (regarding movies, school dances, etc.) in my pre-teen without making him feel like a geek with his friends?

All pre-teen boys feel like geeks. They are easily provoked to do dumb & dangerous things. When I was in 6th grade, I raced my bike down a steep driveway and wound up in a dry creek bed. This stunt earned me three cracked ribs, numerous cuts and bruises, a wrecked bicycle, and lots of ridicule from the guys I was trying to impress. You can help by:

➢ Holding your son to high religious, moral, and academic standards.
➢ Sitting down with his father *privately and regularly* to review activity requirements (like school, church and youth group), limits, curfews, etc.
➢ If dad is gone, getting a close family member or friend to help. When parents are unified and willing to enforce their expectations, kids respond well. When parents are divided and/or unwilling to follow-through, kids slip through the cracks.
➢ Anticipating that your child will claim other parents are not so strict. Your job is to hold your ground, love him fiercely, expect long-term success, and seek family counseling if you feel yourself slipping.

This is a good time to be teaching your children the difference between moral integrity and giving in to peer pressure. Unfortunately, most of us aren't taught this as kids and have to learn it as part of a harder lesson as adults.

➢ Encourage your son to meet other friends from church, Christian youth groups, etc. This is not always a guarantee of integrity so continue to monitor those friendships too.
➢ Offer an environment of open communication to your son.
➢ Allow and encourage him to invite his friends to your home. This will also give you the opportunity to meet his friends.
➢ Explain to your child the reasoning behind the principles you want them to follow. Children will be more receptive if given an explanation rather than an edict of "my way or the highw

***Question 5: My mom never let me do chores
because I never could do them to suit her. My kids
are teenagers and I have done the same to them.
Is it too late to teach them responsibility?***

Parents who do their kids' chores, homework,
etc. are setting them up for a fall. Often, such
parents have an inordinate need to be needed.
They cultivate weakness in their children to make
themselves feel indispensable. Kids raised in this way
eventually feel trapped and smothered. Parents grow
to resent their lazy, dependent children. Anger and
dependence go hand in hand.

To make helpful corrections in the teen years, you
need to:

> ➤ Confess your predicament to God, and ask Him
>   to help you teach your children the importance
>   of work.
> ➤ Insist that they work outside the home for gas
>   and spending money.
> ➤ Agree to pay for basic clothing only and make
>   them pay for the extras.
> ➤ Agree to help with college costs, but do not pay
>   the entire bill.
> ➤ Set a date you will stop subsidizing them and
>   then stop subsidizing them, period.
> ➤ If necessary, get a good family counselor to
>   help you stick to your guns.

Start now. Your mom did you a huge disservice. Your children should be helping out around the house or they will never learn how to take care of themselves and later their own families. Without expecting an allowance, they should do jobs that are age-appropriate, such as clearing the table or putting away their clothes. This is part of living and being a participating member of the household. Giving an allowance should be reserved for jobs that are not part of the daily household tasks. Examples might include washing and cleaning out the car, sweeping out the garage, raking leaves, or polishing silverware. They could also be encouraged to have jobs such as babysitting, mowing, snow shoveling, car washing, paper delivery, etc.

The worst thing parents can do to prepare their kids for the future is to not allow them to work. As a professional, I wouldn't dream of hiring a new college grad that hadn't worked a day in his life. I would choose the uneducated person who had shown work ethic and experience over someone with a degree but no work history.

Question 6: How can a wife be supportive when she disagrees with the way her husband disciplines the children? (Discussion always leads to anger and fights, and nothing gets resolved.)

Most parents disagree on how to discipline the children. As stated earlier, it is important to seal the relational cracks, get help, and remain optimistic. In addition, ask yourself:

> ➤ Is my disagreement vital or trivial? It is wrong to support an alcoholic husband who beats the kids? It is also wrong to withdraw support by refusing to talk or have sexual relations with a husband who yells at the kids and grounds them for a week for breaking a neighbor's window?
> ➤ Am I distinguishing the childrens' needs from my own? A wife may criticize the husband for disciplining a child when she is actually angry that he has been ignoring her. It is important to distinguish between your needs for love and acceptance and the kids' needs for discipline.
> ➤ Am I encouraging my children to reject authority? Lots of parents teach their little angels to ignore instruction unless it is served to their liking. You may believe Dad was too harsh when he confiscated Junior's keys, that the teacher was mistaken to give the poor child an "F" for not doing his homework, or that the manager at Burger King should have warned him not to give away free fries before firing him. In some cases, you may have a valid point. However, Junior needs to know his misbehavior is the problem, not the reaction of the authorities.

If offered, you may want to start with a parenting seminar or workshop at your church. Ask yourself if what you are arguing about is a serious topic such as suspicion of drug or alcohol abuse or is it a trivial issue such as arriving home ten minutes late? If you don't agree on serious issues then you may want to sit down with a school guidance counselor or a trusted advisor.

If the issue is indeed trivial, ask yourself if it is really significant in the grand scheme of raising a child, or are you just being stubborn?

Question 7: I am lucky to be a stay-at-home mom. Why do I feel so discouraged?

You are not lucky. You are blessed. However, with great blessings come great responsibility and tremendous pressure. Your husband, children, extended family and friends demand 110% of your time and energy. You make do with a smaller home, older cars, and fewer dollars than the two-income families down the street. Pastors, the kids' homeroom teachers, friends, and others assume you have nothing but free time on your hands.

In addition, you worry that your professional skills are getting rusty. Former coworkers patronize you, e.g., "How's the little wife doing?" When you try to make a phone call, the kids get into a fight and break something. "No!" becomes your most frequently used word. And your husband, working two jobs and trying to do the home and car repairs himself, has little time to listen to your frustrations.

Under such difficult conditions, discouragement can be expected. To combat it, I recommend that you:

- ➢ Take the long view. Remember that what you are doing is worthwhile and will pay rich dividends in your family members' lives.
- ➢ Trust God. When it is time to return to outside employment, He will meet your needs.
- ➢ Stay current in your profession and/or learn a new one. This may mean taking a class, working outside the home part-time or on contract, and/or developing a home-based business. In any case, the work itself and contact with other adults will stimulate and refresh you.

It is possible your feeling of discouragement comes from isolation. Seek out other stay at home moms. Join Mothers of Preschoolers (MOPS) at a local church, take your kids to the library, get out of the house.

Additionally, you need to find at least an hour or two a week of your own time. Get a manicure, exercise, meet up with friends.

Question 8: My husband has been offered a promotion, but it means a move. Should we do this to our children?

Until forced out by poor health, my parents lived in the house they built when I was four. As a result, I grew up with a firm stick-in-the-mud view toward moving. This has continued into my adult life. My wife and I have lived only in four communities, and we moved our children only once. We follow and recommend the following principles:

> ➤ Make this a religious decision. Ask "Where does God want our family" and honestly seek His guidance in prayer and counsel with trusted Christian friends.
> ➤ Minimize the number of moves, and (if possible) time them to coincide with natural stop/start points in your children's lives. This means moving only when it is necessary, and only when the kids are ready to begin first grade, middle school, high school, and/or college.
> ➤ Don't move solely for money. An increase in salary is not as good for your family as the church, community, and friends you have come to count on.
> ➤ Even if you are in the military service, with a corporation which moves people frequently, or you are "downsized" and have to make an unscheduled or traumatic change, remember: Moving is still *your* decision.

You aren't doing anything to your children. Parents must make the best decision for the overall family. Children are adaptable and can handle moving. Should you move every year just to make a few extra dollars? Probably not, since it is hard to rebuild your support network. However, if the move will take you closer to family/friends then it might be an even better idea.

Moving might actually be good for your children. It will introduce them to new places, teach them how to make new friends, and expand their worlds. They might be presented with better schools, better neighborhoods, and more opportunities to learn and grow. By moving, your children may grow up being less fearful of trying new things, traveling, and exploring new places. Moving does not have to be viewed as a BAD thing.

You might also move your children away from bad influences and have the opportunity for a fresh start somewhere new. Not all children are in love with their school or situation at school. Moving might be an exciting change and fresh start.

Question 9: My parents have offered to buy a car for our 16-year-old son. Should we let them do this?

Some families function openly, with decisions made at the top and communicated clearly and appropriately to the children. Parents and grandparents discuss issues privately. Parents are in charge of their children. Grandparents affirm this and so are able to help without interfering.

Other families function in a clandestine manner. Parents and grandparents have long-standing fundamental disagreements. Parents abdicate responsibility for their children. Grandparents rush to the rescue, joining the children against their parents while claiming, straight-faced, "We were only trying to help."

If you and your spouse are opposed to your son having a car at 16, and/or your parents give with strings attached, and/or your parents first made the offer to your son without consulting you, it might be best to refuse this offer politely. On the other hand, if the following conditions are met, it is possible to accept their proposal:

- ➢ You and your mate have discussed the matter privately and thoroughly.
- ➢ You agree your son is sufficiently skilled and mature to operate an automobile.
- ➢ You have discussed this privately and thoroughly with your parents.
- ➢ Your parents can afford to do so financially.
- ➢ Your parents have a history of helping without interfering.

- ➢ You and your parents understand what is being offered, agree to the details (such as who will pay for gas, insurance, maintenance, etc.)
- ➢ You and your spouse communicate the deal to your son privately.

Question 10: With an 8 month old, I feel like my husband and I are further apart than before our child was born. How do you suggest we get a closer relationship?

You are 100% normal. If you are shocked to hear that, you may have made the common mistake of fantasizing that children add love and intimacy to a marriage. (This may be the underlying fantasy of the teen who becomes pregnant and will not consider giving her child up for adoption. She dreams that the little one will really love her, unlike the boy who lied to her, used her and is pressuring her to get an abortion.)

Children are incredibly demanding. They pump life and love out of their parents. The consideration flows pretty much one way until they become mature adults. Even then, parents still give more than they get. (Note how many adults are moving back in with their aging parents, expecting to live rent free, and borrowing money with no plan for paying it back.)

Whenever I say this publicly, someone spouts-off, "But our children have brought great happiness to our lives!" Praise the Lord, but don't miss the point:

- ➢ Good parents trust God, not their kids, to bring true joy into their lives.
- ➢ Your children may indeed make you proud and happy.
- ➢ However, your job is not to soak up the love, but to ladle it out liberally.

Many couples have a misconception that if they achieve a milestone together, such as buying a house or having a baby, that it will fix their relationship and make them closer. While sometimes this may be a temporary fix, it usually won't be long term. Having a baby is a LOT of work and requires a LOT of patience. This is hard to come by on days when you've been awake several nights with teething, or gas, etc.

If you had issues before the baby was born, you will still have those issues. Work with a counselor to help you. Also, now that the baby is older, find someone you trust to babysit so you and your husband can have time alone together. My husband and I sometimes had a sitter just so we could go grocery shopping together and not have a baby crying.

Question 11: Everything has become about the children, even with our friends. What about us?

This is not selfishness, it is a legitimate concern. It is like the airline rule of putting on your own oxygen mask before putting it on your child. Parents tend to use children to provide a sense of meaning and purpose for the marriage. Healthy couples intentionally discuss their marriage and relationship, knowing that building their own relationship is the best thing they can do for their children.

The concept of "Us" is important and should not be lost. Time alone together, even if it is when the children are in bed sleeping, is valuable. Talk about dreams and goals you have, or set some together. Make time to do things together that you did before you had kids, even simple things like a picnic or a hike alone together.

Try setting aside specific times during the month that you may not discuss anything related to the children. You could even try this with another couple and make it into a game. The first one to bring up something kid-related has to buy dinner!

Question 12: How can we teach our children to avoid the pitfalls we have experienced?

I get that question from parents all the time. For example, they ask, "How can I tell my children not to smoke pot (drink in excess, behave immorally etc.) when I did?" Being a parent with integrity does not mean misleading your children or confessing what you did. It means teaching them to do what is right and sharing what you did only when you believe it is strategically necessarily.

I struggled with this question until Jim and I spoke about it. My first instinct was that I should sit my children down and lay it all out there for them so they can avoid the same mistakes. I believe the better approach is to live my life with integrity and set the example for my children in the present day.

If you used to smoke but stopped (and you aren't sneaking cigarettes in the back yard at midnight), then you don't have to worry about the fact that you used to smoke. It is harder to tell your children why they shouldn't do something that you are still doing. If you are an alcoholic and tell your children drinking is wrong, yet you come home drunk all the time, you lack the moral authority and integrity behind your assertion.

Question 13: When is grown- up honesty too much for children? For example, my spouse is a recovering addict. At what age should we explain this to our children?

1. Take the 12-step approach (a proven method of treatment for various addictions). You have been honest with God, yourself and at least one other person, preferably your spouse. That is the beginning of integrity and you are no longer pretending.

2. Evaluate your children's readiness for grown- up-style information. This issue often arises in the context of divorce or remarriage.

3. Tell children the truth, but first make sure you are responding to what they are actually asking. A lot of times children aren't really asking what you think they are. "Mommy, why did you divorce daddy?" might really be, "Mommy, will daddy come to my birthday party Saturday?" It is vital to ask the follow-up question first, then give an absolutely truthful, age-appropriate answer.

Ditto.

Question 14: Should we talk to and/or involve our children in our marriage counseling?

No. Healthy parenting means that the kids are wondering what you are up to. Unhealthy parenting means you are wondering what the kids are up to.

Ditto.

Question 15: My spouse and I have been fighting. Our son has always been a model child. Now we are getting calls from school about his poor behavior. I believe he is responding to the tension in our home. What should we do?

Theoretically, keep the focus on your child's behavior. Develop plans for enforcing good behavior and cooperate on getting that done. You also need to address your financial issues in a way that solves them rather than creating additional tension in your home. This may include seeing a financial counselor or a trusted financial person from your church. In any case, resolve this for your child's sake.

I agree with Jim. An additional thought is when you discuss this, do so at another location or out of earshot of the children. For example, my husband and I wait until our children are in bed to have serious discussions that we don't want our children to hear.

Question 16: My ex and I have three teenage children. They are asking me why we broke up. What can I share that will help them learn from our experience? My ex is still very bitter about our separation.

Ask your children, "What do you really want to know?" Then answer in an honest way that will not antagonize your ex.
 Don't try to do too much too fast. Model good communication.   Make sure they see something other than bitterness and brokenness in your home.   When they are older they will reflect what you have taught them about relationships.

Be as honest as you can without bashing the other parent to make yourself seem like a victim.   Try and frame it in the most benevolent manner possible yet sharing with your children concepts of why your marriage may not have worked out. Perhaps it was youth, jumped into the marriage quickly, ignored signs of incompatibility before marriage, addiction issues, differences in maturity levels.

Question 17: My husband's ex-wife provokes conflict between my husband and me. For example, she changes schedules at the last minute and it creates chaos for our family. We end up fighting. Why does he take his anger out on me?

This sort of passive-aggressive sabotage is common. It is important to understand that disrupting your marriage, i.e., not working out scheduling conflicts, can be the ex-spouse's goal. Refuse to allow your ex-spouse this power! Instead, work through the scheduling problems as best you can, and then share your frustration with your spouse in a non-attacking, non-defensive manner.

Your spouse is probably angry and doesn't want to create additional conflict with his ex. It seems that many divorced men walk on eggshells trying to remain friendly with their exes out of some guilt related to not being with their child. They don't want to rock the boat. Unfortunately, it seems to perpetuate the issue. This is not healthy for any family. Your husband needs to stand up for your family so the ex will cease messing with the schedule.

Question 18: My husband pushes our children to excel in sports. Our son is a very gifted musician and doesn't have much interest in sports but plays to please my husband. How can I get through to my husband that not everyone needs to participate in sports?

It is possible your son enjoys both sports and music but is complaining to you to provoke disunity between you and his father. Children do this routinely and it makes decision making more difficult. Ask him to work this out with his father and be careful you don't see yourself as rescuing him from a cruel and dictatorial dad. Later, discuss this with your husband to determine the situation was actually what your son described.

I need to disagree. Both moms and dads can get caught up in these obsessions about their child's success. Wanting their kids to succeed often means parents cannot discern between their desires and their children's talents, gifts and desires. It becomes what the parent wants their child to be. Children should be exposed to a variety of activities so their talents can rise to the top. I agree with Jim that you should discuss this privately with your husband.

Dialogue: What About Joe?

Susan called Monday for an appointment.

"Joe and I have a blended family, and we need help."

I answered, "Can you come over tonight at around seven?"

Susan countered, "No, we can't. We both work. Could you see us at 7 on Saturday night?" Against my better judgment, I ignored what was probably an insult and made the appointment.

At 7:45 p.m. Saturday, an expensive German sedan pulled into the church lot and parked next to my car. I greeted the family at the front door and led them down the hallway to my private office. No one apologized for being late, or for imposing on prime family time.

Joe and Susan, an attractive couple in their mid-40s, chose the couch, while Susan's daughter Beth, a very mature-looking 17-year-old in jeans and a college sweatshirt, claimed the folding chair nearest the door. Joe's son Max, a skinny 14-year-old "skater" with baggy jeans drooping down to his knees, his bottom barely covered by a huge rap- group T-shirt, slipped behind my desk and plopped into the swivel chair. "Cool!" he said, pushing away from the desk and spinning around. "I think I'm gonna hurl!"

I waited for Joe and/or Susan to ask the boy to come out from behind the desk and join the group, but they smiled and said nothing. I sat down beside Beth and, facing Joe and Susan, asked, "How can I help you?" Behind me, I could hear Max punching the buttons on my desk phone.

Susan said she was disturbed about her daughter's plan to drop out of school and move in with her 25-year-old boyfriend. "Whatever," Beth responded, rolling her eyes and turning away from her mother.

Susan began to cry. Joe smiled awkwardly.

Apparently tired of spinning around in my chair, Max started going through my desk drawers. "Do you keep any money in here? I want a can of pop."

No longer able to ignore his son's behavior, Joe said weakly, "Now, Max, anything you take will come out of your allowance."

Dialogue Starters:
➢ What do you think prevents Joe and Susan from giving their children the discipline they obviously need?
➢ What do you believe can be done to strengthen this marriage?
➢ What kind of spiritual leadership do you think Joe can exercise in his family?

Dialogue: Children in the Mix

After 15 years of marriage, Peter and Jeanine had four children, ages 14, 11, 7 and 5. They moved to a new town when their youngest had just started kindergarten. Jeanine, a physical therapist, stayed at home once they began having children. From the outside looking in, this family had it all. They had a nice house, drove nice cars, went on vacations, and attended church. Their children were involved in a variety of sports and activities. Peter was a big shot executive for a consulting firm and was on the road most weeks. After the move, Jeanine had fewer friends, was always running the children here and there and did not have time for herself. She began drinking in the evenings when the kids were in bed to help her relax from the day. She often said, "One drink would not hurt anyone". When Peter was home on the weekends he would spend all his time either playing sports with their sons or sitting in front of the TV watching sports. It didn't matter what season it was, if there was a sport on TV, he watched it.

As the years went by Jeanine drank more in the evenings and on the weekends and soon she was having alcohol during the day when the kids were in school. She was sure her husband was unfaithful because she had not had his attention in years.

Mom and dad stayed together "for the kids". As soon as the kids were out of school the plan was to divorce.

One by one the children left for college. When the youngest was nearing the end of his senior year, Peter and Jeanine split up. Peter almost immediately had a 20-something girlfriend and Jeanine felt old, alone and miserable. She had not worked outside the home in over 25 years and her life had been centered around her children's activities and alcohol. As her children grew up and moved away she was along and a bottle became her life.

Dialogue Starters:
➢ Was it better for the parents to stay together for the children?
➢ How could they have worked on their relationship?
➢ Should parents try to hide marital issues from their children for long periods of time?

Question 19: My spouse and I are empty nesters. The holidays are around the corner and our daughter is going on vacation with her friends. Should I confront her about this and tell her how upset her dad and I are that she is not coming home?

This kind of confrontation is a form of punishment. Unless she already agreed to come home, and is therefore breaking a promise, she has done nothing wrong. If she is out of school and established in her own home, it is even more inappropriate to criticize her for living her own life. It is better to ask when she might be able to make the trip, or plan a holiday trip in her area and offer to take her out to eat. Let her invite you to her place if she desires. Make every attempt to support her for her independent living, rather than making her feel guilty about it.

I would ask you to consider three different scenarios and see if you can relate to any of them:
1. My expectations are too high and cause strained relationships.
2. I often give our kids a guilt trip when they call or send emails. I believe this is keeping them away.
3. My spouse or I have an addiction issue and over-indulge during the holidays. This can lead to uncomfortable visits with the family.

Question 20: My parents are divorced and both remarried. They are amicable, yet I still notice some jealousy, especially related to their time with the grandkids. We don't mean to favor either set of grandparents. How do we handle this?

Gently make it clear that you intend to divide time as equally as possible. Often, this means alternating "favor" from one set to the other (e.g. Christmas morning with one set this year, and next year with the other.) This can be complicated by other factors (e.g., one set of grandparents drinks excessively, lives especially far away, or is especially demeaning and critical.) In the long run, develop your own nuclear family traditions and work the grandparents in as best you can.

Since your parents are amicable, I would say invite them all for important events and holidays.

Question 21: My husband pays support, alimony and other expenses of his ex-wife. However, when the ex sends the kids to our house for new sports equipment, school supplies, shoes, coats etc., he obliges. We are struggling to pay our own bills and afford similar items for our other children. He lets her manipulate him which leads to arguments between us. Why can't he say no and stand up for our family?

The husband probably thinks he is keeping the peace, yet his behavior creates disharmony. He needs to learn to say, "I will continue to meet my obligations, but I expect you to use some of the child support money to pay for these 'extras'." You can help him by understanding the bind he is in and appreciating his generosity and love for his children. He also needs to learn to stall—to avoid saying "Yes" too fast and peeling out money without thinking about the consequences. He needs to think, "Does my child really need these items?" and "How can I help my child to earn part or all of the money to purchase them?"

I believe this is "divorced dad guilt". I have seen this happen more times than I can count from men of all ages and economic circumstances. Many men want to keep the peace with their ex because they believe it will make things easier.

The dad does not want the confrontation and does not want the mother to turn the child against him. The dad kowtows to his ex's every whim even to the detriment of the rest of the family. In the end, it rarely helps the situation and instead creates a spiral affect.

The ex realizes she can demand and get away with anything without consequence. She knows all she has to do is threaten court or threaten the dad's time with his children. Much of this may be due to a justice system that, without costly attorney fees, does not adequately protect the father's rights.

The impact this type of "relationship" between the parents has on the children often backfires later in life. When the children reach adulthood and see the same thing happen to their own friends who divorce, many will realize that their mother was not the martyr saint and the father the scumbag as she portrayed him. This often leads to a new compassion for the father and disillusionment toward the mother. This nasty cycle has potential to ruin the grown child's relationships as well.

Chapter 4   Communication

Question 1: **How do you keep things "fresh and new" (i.e., fight off the routine and stay out of the rut?)**

Question 2: **If a wife has trouble confronting her parents, can the husband help do the confronting?**

Question 3: **My husband knows much of what transpired in my family in the past but I have not shared some of the gruesome details. Is it okay to keep negative things from your spouse if it will preserve family relationships?   I love my family and I don't want my spouse to judge them.**

Question 4: **Why do some men spend so much time and energy on their job instead of their family, and why don' t they see they are doing it?**

Question 5: **What tips do you have for making the world back off so we can spend more time together?**

Question 6: **How do you find time to be alone with your husband while taking care of four children, a house, and being involved in church ministries?**

Question 7: **What do you do when one person always wants to "be together" and can't understand why the other person doesn't feel the same way?**

Question 8: **My spouse won't stop gossiping. All I hear about is what the neighbors are doing and** *who said what and who is doing what etc. I can't take it anymore. Why can't we talk about something else?*

Question 9: *My spouse doesn't listen to me. I get angry that my opinion isn't considered. This is causing me to lose respect for my spouse because I don't feel like my thoughts/ideas/suggestions are respected. What can I do about it?*

Communication

A few years ago, a couple arrived for marital counseling. I asked, "So how do you hope I can help you?" The man said "I love my wife. I want to save our marriage." Without blinking an eye, his wife said "I want a divorce. My lawyer has already filed the papers. I am here only to discuss the best way to help our children during this difficult time." The husband smiled weakly and squeaked, "I guess we have a have a communication problem."

I thought their communication was quite clear. He wanted in, and she wanted out. As the hour wore on, it became apparent that he was clinging to the "communication problem" like a shipwrecked sailor clings to floating debris. He just *knew* that if she really understood him, she would change her mind.

This man, and many others like him, use the term "communication problem" to sidestep the moral, ethical, and religious matters which really separate them. They need to know that clarity does not ensure unity, and that malice is not simply a misunderstanding.

Godly communication is clear but it is also Christ-like. "I hate you" is better said: "I cultivate hatred toward you to justify my sinful desire to abandon you". We are striving toward true repentance. I hope you find the following answers helpful in improving your marital communication.

Question 1: How do you keep things "fresh and new"? (i.e., fight off the routine and stay out of the rut)

If you raise this issue in a Bible school class or small group, you'll get some great ideas.

However, I think the best bet is to associate with some "fresh and new" people. If you are like most folks, you have limited your friendships to persons who are about your age and income level who share your views. Here are a few ideas:

> Try a "working-adventure-getaway" with your spouse, such as a short-term mission trip to Haiti, Mexico, or even Eastern Europe.
> Volunteer at a crisis pregnancy center, a local nursing home, or your child's school.
> Invite someone from whom you would ordinarily shy away from to dinner…perhaps someone who is richer, poorer, whiter, or blacker than you are.
> Discover that differences can be delightful!

Shake things up. We all fall into ruts and routines. The ideas above are just a few examples of new things to add to your life that you and your spouse can share together.

Question 2: If a wife has trouble confronting her parents, can the husband help do the confronting?

Yes, but this must be done in close consultation and agreement with his wife. Many husbands (and wives, too) have rushed in to rescue a spouse who doesn't really want or need to be rescued. I suggest you try discussing the following issues with your wife:

> How serious is the offense? Confronting a spouse's parent with something serious like alcohol abuse, child molestation, or some other criminal behavior might be worth the effort. Confronting them with something minor, such as eccentric habits or taste in clothing is not.
> Is it any of your business? For example, you may not like that your wife's parents decide to give all of their money to the city zoo. But it is their money and their business, not yours. Stay out of it!
> Will they listen to you? It is a complete waste of time and breath to continue confronting them if they don't want to hear. If what they are doing is illegal, call the police. If it is immoral, limit the time you and your kids spend with them. However, in general, mind your own business and stay out of theirs.

Yes, if the issue is worth confronting the parents, but only if both husband and wife agree that this needs to be done. If your parents are planning on downsizing, moving, changing jobs, getting remarried...mind your own business.

An example may be the way the parents are influencing your children. If you left your children at their house last weekend and found out they let your children have their friends over for a party and served alcohol, then you absolutely have every right as a parent to confront your in-laws. However, if they served too much cake and ice cream, that may be a time for you to keep quiet. If in general, your kids are safe, then you may want to understand that the grandparents are going to make decisions about diet and other things may not align with yours. If something they do is very egregious, you can limit the time that your children are around them.

Another example: If your wife hears from her sister that their parents are thinking of selling their house to downsize and the daughters are upset about this decision, then no, you shouldn't confront them. Mind your own business.

Question 3: My husband knows much of what transpired in my family in the past but I have not shared some of the gruesome details. Is it okay to keep negative things from your spouse if it will preserve family relationships? I love my family and I don't want my spouse to judge them.

 Combined Answer Jim and Shawna : If one of your relatives represents a moral threat or safety concern, then you need to be completely forthcoming. However, past family situations are often considered confidential or private. A broad overview, e.g., "My dad drank heavily and was cruel to my mom", is sufficient. A blow-by-blow description of your father's profanity laced drunken tirades is unnecessary and may needlessly sabotage a growing healthy relationship between your spouse and your father. A compulsive need to tell all may have less to do with honesty and more to do with fear and anxiety.

Question 4: Why do some men spend so much time and energy on their job instead of their family, and why don't they see they are doing it?

I assume the men you mention are working, and that they are so consumed by productive labor that they have little time or energy for anything else. To answer this question, it is good to begin with the biblical theology of work.

God created Adam to tend His Garden. In that pristine, sin-free world, human work was perfectly productive. Crops grew weed-free. But when Adam rebelled, God punished him by rendering his labor less productive. Weeds infested the wheat, forcing a hungry Adam to cultivate or starve. By God's grace, the earth continued to respond to Man's labor. But under God's curse, pain now accompanied the grain.

God not only called Man to work, but to rest. First by example and then by Law, God established the Sabbath Day of rest. Jesus observed the Sabbath, taught that it was made for Man's benefit, and often retreated to the mountains for relaxation. From cover to cover, God's Word calls us to a redemptive, balanced life of productive labor punctuated by rest and relaxation.

By working too much, a man (or woman) joins Adam in rebellion against God and His created order. The so-called workaholic is not an addict. He is a sinner. Perhaps you can underline this section and leave it at your man's office or place of business. Let him know that, through work, he can never:

➢ Make himself feel worthy.
➢ Earn his way to heaven.
➢ Ensure his future through material gain.
➢ Avoid his other God-given responsibilities.

As to why they don't see it, I believe it is EGO! Men's jobs define them. If the man is the primary breadwinner, there is the unspoken burden that they must provide for the family and must not fail. Men do not want to fail their families, but some of them don't realize that not being around is a form of failure. They may have been raised in a similar environment and this is what they are used to. .

Question 5: What tips do you have for making the world back off so we can spend more time together?

"The world is too much with us; late and soon, getting and spending, we lay waste our powers." So said the great poet of England, William Wordsworth, in about 1800. From Adam to the Atomic Age, men and women have struggled with this problem. I suggest the following:

> - In your Sunday school class or small group, discuss the question "When I am on my deathbed, upon what will I look back with joy?" and record the answers.
> - Visit the nearest nursing home and ask a few seasoned saints, "Now that you are old, what memories give you the most joy?" Record their answers.
> - Check your list against theirs.
> - Live accordingly!

You need to carve out time to be together. If that means missing a Sunday football game to have dinner together, then that should be the priority. In general, it is a wise decision to turn off the TV. Spend the time instead with your spouse and/or your children. Read together, goof around, tell stories, play games, talk about the day or your plans for the weekend.

Question 6: How do you find time to be alone with your husband while taking care of four children, a house, and being involved in church ministries?

We have already spoken to the issues of romance, renewing passion, showing love with the kids around, etc. Let me make a few points and recommendations concerning church involvement and the Christian couple.

> Being alone with your mate (that is, enjoying and improving your marital intimacy) is more important than getting the kids to their activities, vacuuming the carpet, or attending a church committee meeting.
> Marital intimacy is enhanced by mutual, regular participation in worship, fellowship, Christian education, small group participation, and ministry.
> If you are run ragged by church activities, it is time to admit that the church has become part of the problem rather than part of the solution.
> Don't drop out. Meet with your pastors, ministers, and youth leaders and help them understand your needs as a family.
> Wean yourself from the rash of activities that are helping you avoid a sane, happy family life.

In addition to the points above, regarding housework: Sometimes 'house issues' just need to wait. Maybe you dust once every two weeks instead of every week and you let the dishes sit one night after dinner or use disposable plates so you have that extra time to spend with your husband.

Question 7: What do you do when one person always wants to "be together" and can't understand why the other person doesn't feel the same way?

Your spouse might have grown up in a household which quietly yet severely punished independent thought and action. Non-family members were treated as "outsiders" to be placated and avoided. Insiders proved their loyalty by remaining over-involved in family matters. Dating, marriage, and even having children were emotionally approved only if everyone 'folded' back into this 'batter'.

When you act independently in any regard, you break the family rules. Your spouse says, "I can't understand why" not because he/she really can't understand, but because he/she really does not approve of your actions. A good marital therapist can help you understand these dynamics and teach you to provide the reassurance your spouse needs to "leave and cleave."

If you are a stay-at-home parent and don't have your own outside activities, when your spouse comes home from work, he becomes your primary source of entertainment and relief from the kids. You have been craving adult companionship all day and now you just want to be with your spouse.

It is healthy to want to spend time together. It is also healthy to have activities or events that you each might do individually. Once a month your husband could watch the kids so you can go for a manicure or to lunch with some friends. Volunteer or find activities to give you adult interaction so your spouse isn't your sole form of companionship.

Realize that your spouse will also want to spend time with friends, even alone. There should be a healthy balance. Alternatively, if the two of you just don't enjoy each other's company anymore and it has become an issue of avoidance, then you should consider counseling.

Question 8: My spouse won't stop gossiping. All I hear about is what the neighbors are doing and who said what and who is doing what etc. I can't take it anymore. Why can't we talk about something else?

When my wife and I were first married, we talked too much about other people and things and not enough about our own thoughts about each other. Things were too 'third person' and not enough 'first person'. One solution might be to try spending less time speaking in the third person (he, she, they, etc.) and more time in the first person (I. me, us, etc.).

For example: less 'he said, she said', and more 'I think, I want, I hope…'

An inability to speak in first person indicates a lack of marital intimacy. Refer to our section of marital intimacy to increase that aspect of your life.

It does seem some people thrive on gossip. Perhaps they are lacking substance in their own life. Try talking with your spouse about what is going on with her life, her day to day tasks. The gossip may stem from routine boredom or an escape mechanism.

Let your spouse know that you want to talk with her and listen to her about things that are important in her life. Try coming up with a list of questions you can ask her each day to drive the conversation away from other people. Be sure she knows that you care about what she has to say and that you want to listen to her but you would like to discuss other topics.

Proverbs 16:28: "A perverse man stirs up dissension, and a gossip separates close friends."

90

Question 9: My spouse doesn't listen to me. I get angry that my opinion isn't considered. This is causing me to lose respect for my spouse because I don't feel like my thoughts/ideas/suggestions are respected. What can I do about it?

From a personal standpoint, I have found over the years that my wife is right about a lot of things. It irritates me that she thinks of things that I didn't. It challenges my identity as a man and a spiritual leader. It forces me to adopt a different model of leadership in my home.

First, not saying 'I told you so' is a good idea. Instead, I can say I am often wrong have no reason to put someone down when they are wrong.
Secondly, leadership is often how you respond to a situation rather than who is right and who is wrong.

My grandfather was someone who could press his point, and whether he was right or wrong, could behave in the next moment as if there was never a conflict.

Talking about the specific issue is one thing but talking about the *way* we talk is part of the solution as well.

Conversation with your spouse may be: "Have you noticed that when I suggest something, I sense from the way you respond or don't respond that you don't really respect my thoughts on it?"

This is an area where a marriage counselor or enrichment teacher can help with slowing down communication and encouraging each person to give specific feedback. Sometimes just slowing things down and asking people to repeat what they heard can communicate additional respect. We give feedback to those we respect.

This can be an issue with both genders. It is important to discuss how this is making you feel with your spouse. If they are unwilling to listen, try writing a letter explaining how you feel. If your spouse is not open to trying to understand how you are feeling you should consider meeting with a counselor.

Chapter 5 Money

Question 1: **Should a wife have a career outside the home, or be a full-time homemaker and mother?**

Question 2: **How can I find a good balance between home, family, church, and school activities? As a stay-at-home mom, I often feel overloaded.**

Question 3: **Now that I have a child, should I leave my career and be a full-time mom, trusting the finances to God? How can I determine what is the appropriate amount of attention for my child?**

Question 4: **How can a couple work in their own business successfully 24 hours a day, 7 days a week, and stay happily married?**

Question 5: **We are sick of paying rent, but we believe it is wrong to go in debt to purchase a house. What should we do?**

Question 6: **My wife is a compulsive shopper and justifies it by buying things on "sale". I just found out she has several store credit cards of which I was unaware. How can I help her understand what this is doing to our finances and our relationship?**

Question 7: **We can afford our house but didn't realize all the other expenses that come with it. Many stores offer "buy today and pay later" with no interest. I think we should furnish our home. My spouse disagrees. What should we do?**

Question 8: My spouse and I own a small business. The last year has been financially difficult. All we talk and fight about is money. How can we maintain a healthy perspective on this?

Money

The first and best way to ensure financial stability and career success is simple: *Carry minimum consumer debt.* God will bless you with the income you need. And when He calls you to change jobs, relocate, go back to school, stay home with the kids, go part-time or go full-time, you will be free to follow His leading. When economic times are bad, you will survive. When times are good, you will prosper.

Many Christians ignore this simple, biblical truth. They want nice cars, furniture, meals out, and vacations, but they want them *now.* So they borrow, spend, borrow more, work like dogs to make the payments, invite stress-induced illnesses, and fight constantly about money. Hooked on a higher lifestyle than they can afford, they become slaves to the creditors who feed their addiction.

This addiction spurs irrational thought and behavior. I have worked with scores of unemployed Christians who claim they cannot find work, yet when confronted, become defensive and admit, "With two car payments, charge cards, and school loans, I can't afford to take just *anything.*" Sinking fast by the bow into the depths of financial ruin, they pretend they are still in command. Their delusion is reinforced by the saving stream of credit cards and 125% home equity loan solicitations which arrive every day in the mail.

Corporations make the same mistake. Employers who run their companies primarily on leveraged capital (borrowed money) need an uninterrupted and ever-increasing cash flow to satisfy their creditors and make a profit. During normal "dips" in the business cycle, they survive by juggling accounts payable, stalling creditors, rumoring, reorganizing, and downsizing.

These tactics sweeten the bottom line for a quarter or two, but sabotage the firm's long-term viability.
The following questions are tough enough without the specter of bankruptcy hovering just overhead. The decision to live within one's means is the first and most important step to answering career-related questions.

Question 1: Should a wife have a career outside the home, or be a full-time homemaker and mother?

Career decisions are best made by a married couple in consultation with a pro-family pastor. I do not know your situation, but I can share our family's approach.

Though it meant living on a small church preacher's salary, we decided that I would work full-time and she would stay home with our children, at least until they were both in elementary school. We lived in a smaller home than most of our church members, vacationed in a worn-out pop-up camping trailer someone gave us, drove cars until they dropped, avoided the use of credit, and still "tithed" 10% of our gross income to the church.

My wife returned to teaching when our younger child was in 2nd grade. When we moved to Indianapolis, she stayed home a year to stabilize our then teenagers. Because we carried no consumer debt, we were able to get by on one meager, fluctuating income.

We still live in a modest home and drive older cars. We avoid using credit cards. When we do, we pay the entire balance at the end of each month. God has blessed us financially. Most importantly, we have two children who know that they are our first priority.

Being a full time parent is a wonderful opportunity if your situation allows it and it is something you want to do. I would encourage you to become involved in Mothers of Preschooler (MOPS), charitable activities, volunteer opportunities, etc. If you are a professional who wants to stay home for a few years, you may want to join an organization to keep up with the industry and network opportunities.

I would also highly encourage you to understand the family finances, have a list of all your financial obligations, account numbers, passwords, etc. I have seen too many women lose a spouse and be totally lost in this area.

A stay- at- home mom sometimes believes that staying at home is a promise her husband made to her. But if he loses his job or his hours are cut, it can create real crisis in the household. A wife need to evaluate how to make ends meet. Sometimes at this moment it is more important to survive than to force the husband's hand. Address the issue of financial emergency.

Question 2: How can I find a good balance between home, family, church, and school activities? As a stay-at-home mom, I often feel overloaded.

For moms who feel overloaded, I recommend the following:

➢ Look in the mirror and meet the person who most overloads you.
➢ Understand that God's goodness and mercy are chasing you. Slow down and let them catch up!
➢ Share these concerns with your husband and ask for his prayers and support.
➢ Team up with other moms for prayer and peer-group accountability. Soon you will be able to say a firm "Yes!" to the activities which fit, and a polite "No" to those which don't.

You need to have some time for yourself to reflect and clear your mind. Have your husband or a friend watch your kids so you can go for a walk or run. Have a 'ladies night' or a tea with friends once a month. Try to work out car pools with other parents or one night a week when you eat on disposable plates. Teach your children responsibilities such as putting away their clothes, taking dirty clothes to the laundry, or putting dishes in the sink. All of these little things will add time back into your day and teach your children what responsibility is.

Question 3: Now that I have a child, should I leave my career and be a full-time mom, trusting the finances to God? How can I determine what is the appropriate amount of attention for my child?

Before stumbling into this minefield, let me share three neglected precepts. First, *a career is a path, not a profession.* Your journey to faith, marriage, and motherhood are God-ordained portions of your career, not diversions from it. Second, *trust is a must.* Your financial well-being is in God's hands regardless of your employment status. Third, *attention is a matter of moments.* The more time you invest, the more once-in-a-lifetime redemptive moments you (and *only* you) can share with your child.

The Christian path is marked by sacrifice and courage. I know church families who live on one income, juggle work schedules to maximize time with their children, work flex- or part-time, nights, weekends, holidays, etc. Solutions vary, but the goal is the same: To accept children as a gift from God and raise them to know Him. If this is your goal, you should:

➢ Contact your pastor, see a good Christian counselor, and discuss these matters with couples who have faced similar challenges.
➢ Watch for opportunities to join a Christian financial accountability group. More churches are offering these to help their members set a godly course and stick to it.

You cannot give your children too much attention. You can give them too much bad attention. Positive attention such as reading and singing to your children is a good thing. Smothering them and not allowing them to explore and grow is bad.

If you are in a financial position to leave your career AND you wish to do so, then yes, stay at home. But don't randomly quit your job without understanding the full implications to your financial situation. Yes, God provides, but he may have provided you with the ability to have the career so that you can provide for your family. You need to evaluate the situation and determine what makes the most sense for your family.

Maybe you will discover that the cost of daycare will about equal your pay and that you would rather raise your children than have someone else do so. In this case, it doesn't make sense to keep working if you can afford not to.

Alternatively, once you have children able to help with the family finances, you may find that you only need to work part- time. Sit down with your spouse and write out a list of all of your expenses. Include a buffer for unforeseen expenses. Then figure out if you will have the money needed to cover those expenses if you aren't working. If the answer is no, go back through the list and identify items that you can eliminate. Can you eliminate a daily trip to Starbucks? Or can you pack a lunch for your husband instead of his eating out every day? You will not have the same expenses for work clothes and everything that goes along with a career but you will have costs, such as diapers, associated with having children. Can you eliminate or decrease enough from your list?

One reason couples wind up divorced is the strain on a relationship caused by money mismanagement. It isn't fun to have your car repossessed in the middle of the night or being afraid to answer the phone because it may be a debt collector.

Question 4: How can a couple work in their own business successfully 24 hours a day, 7 days a week and stay happily married?

I don't know, but "24 hours a day, 7 days a week" sounds somewhat out-of-balance. Couples who run time-intensive businesses like farms and restaurants need time away to concentrate on their marriage. Try contracting with someone else to mind the business and take some time away. The overhead will go up a little, but the long-term stability of the business and the marriage will be enhanced.

You need to have separation of work and personal life. Set aside time every day to talk with your spouse about anything that is NOT related to the business. Turn it into a game: don't even mention the business. I have heard of people using the "swear jar" technique. Here is how it works: when you vocalize a topic that is off limits you have to toss an agreed-upon-dollar amount into the jar, $.50 or $1. You can save this money up and use it for a date night.

Question 5: We are sick of paying rent, but we believe it is wrong to go in debt to purchase a house. What should we do?

If you lease an apartment, you are in debt. You are borrowing a place to live, obligated for the length of the lease, and vulnerable to arbitrary rent increases. I think it is wise to buy a house. Here's why:

If you have a healthy down payment (e.g. 20%), buy a modest home in a good location, and maintain the home carefully, the increase in value and the benefit of tax advantages make it a wise investment. By making an extra payment or two per year, you can chop several years off the mortgage and save thousands of dollars in interest.

Of course, you can lose. Your house may decrease in value. You may lose your job and be unable to make payments. The economy may collapse. However, you have to live somewhere, and a comparable apartment will cost nearly the same amount. All things considered, it is best to buy a modest, affordable home, maintain it well, and pay it off as soon as possible.

Here's a caveat: Buying too much house can ruin you financially, particularly if you are counting on two uninterrupted, ever-increasing incomes and monetary inflation (the government printing of baseless, progressively worthless money) to ease the pain. Some rules of thumb may be helpful:

> ➤ Spend no more than 25% of your primary monthly income for housing (includes principle and interest).

- Be content with a smaller, more easily maintained home than those in which your friends live.
- Use the cost and time savings to benefit your children and church.
- Plan for the day when you may have to keep going on a single income.

There are two kinds of debt, good and bad. Good debt generally includes appreciating assets and bad debt includes depreciating assets. Homeownership is an investment if done properly. A new boat is not an investment. Rent is not an investment either. Be careful not to spend all of your money on depreciating assets.

I would like to add a concept to this section called delayed gratification. I was very fortunate to be raised by a family full of entrepreneurs and small business owners. I say that because they taught me the concept of delayed gratification. Even knowing the concept, I have slipped here and there along the way. Set goals for yourself and your family.

Question 6: My wife is a compulsive shopper and justifies it by buying things on "sale". I just found out she has several store credit cards of which I was unaware. How can I help her understand what this is doing to our finances and our relationship?

I worked for a church once that was always "saving money" by not buying needed equipment, expanding building, etc. I always wondered, "Just where is all this money we have been saving?" Old-timers would have called them "skinflints" –a flintlock firearm metaphor denoting a soldier who endangers himself by using flints which have worn thin and can fail at a critical moment.

This question presents the photographic negative version of the same problem. This lady (and guys do it too) might be called a "Spendthrift" – an oxymoron denoting a person who believes purchasing items at some real or imagined discount actually saves money.

Be straightforward and loving. Tell her this is not frugality, but an attempt to fill an empty place in her heart. Tell her that this is a trust issue – that your "one flesh" relationship demands that you agree on important matters such as how to use credit. Review all of your credit statements personally, and set a plan to pay them off. If necessary, consult a credit counselor.

This can be a serious problem, even when the person in question can afford the things she is buying. Sit down with your wife and write down all of your expenses, including money set aside for savings, retirement funds, tithing or donations. Then discuss what your family financial goals are for the short term as well as for retirement purposes. This process alone may help your spouse realize that while she loves to get a good deal, limits should be set on the spending to help achieve the family's financial goals.

Let your wife know how this situation is making you feel. Many times people shop to help fill a void in their lives or to make themselves feel better about something. You may tell her that you appreciate her determination to 'save' money by scoping out the best deals, but that you would rest easier at night not having credit card debt.

As for the credit cards you were unaware of, this may be an innocent by- product of our shopping experiences today. Almost every store offers savings today if we sign up for their credit card. They also send special advance sale notices and coupons or gift cards to keep you coming back. This plays on the desire to get a 'good deal'. I am not excusing the habit of reckless spending or having a bunch of credit cards that you can't afford, but in your wife's mind she may not have been thinking it was a secret when she signed up for the cards but rather just a normal part of the shopping experience.

Question 7: We can afford our house but didn't realize all the other expenses that come with it. Many stores offer "buy today and pay later" with no interest. I think we should furnish our home. My spouse disagrees. What should we do?

This sounds like you have a lot of 'wants' for your new home, not necessarily needs. Sit down together and write out a list of all of the things you would like to buy for your new home. Then go through it and categorize everything by importance with this in mind:, You can ONLY pick one item per month. Once you have done that you should start to see what is more on the 'need' side than 'want'. If your new home didn't come with a stove, then this is obviously a higher priority than getting a new TV for the kids' play room. Determine how much of the monthly finances will be dedicated to this list.

This is where the concept I mentioned earlier comes into play: delayed gratification. People used to work hard and save their pennies. When they could afford to pay in full, they bought things. They would save and save for weeks, months, or years so they could buy what they wanted.

You need to be careful with the buy now/pay later offers. The way many of them work is that you have 6 months or longer of no payments and no interest. The catch is that if you haven't paid in that time period they charge you for ALL of the interest. So you really haven't saved anything over charging it on a regular credit card.

I have used these deals myself for new appliances, and they can be a great way to make purchases like that if you are disciplined. I figure out the amount I need to pay every month so that I can pay it off before the end of the free interest term. If you are not a disciplined person when it comes to credit then I don't recommend this option.

Credit cards don't have to be a bad thing. I use mine for just about everything and have points accumulate. The caveat is, I have always paid them off every month. I don't have a running balance. The joke is that it has lowered my exceptional credit score because I don't carry revolving debt. However, I would rather take a slight hit on the credit score than pay those exorbitant interest rates and fees. They do make commerce much easier. As an example, when you call to make a reservation for travel they ask for your credit card. It is the way the world does business now. And ironically, even though credit cards can hurt your credit score by paying them off every month, they also help your score just by having them.

An alternative exists today that allows you to use your debit card like a credit card. This allows you to use it in all of the same places that you would a regular credit card but the money is immediately removed from your bank account. This means you should not be accumulating debt on a credit card and paying high interest rates and fees.

I am going to defer to my young friend because she has covered the topic and I agree with what she has written.

Question 8: My spouse and I own a small business. The last year has been financially difficult. All we talk and fight about is money. How can we maintain a healthy perspective on this?

When Linda and I faced times like this, I had to realize three facts of life:

1) I need her. I need her love, support, and encouragement. Specifically, I need her to reassure me that she will help me succeed, make our home a happy place, and help earn part of our living through wise household management and/or working outside the home.

2) I cannot push my point to the point that it permanently divides us. If she is worried, screaming at her or threatening to leave can only make things worse.

3) She needs my reassurance—honest, realistic promises to work hard, work smart, and be frugal.

One or both of you should look at finding a job, if only as a temporary situation until you can get your business back on track financially. Sit down together and come up with a plan for getting work expenses under control. Revisit your business plan to see what you need to do to turn things around. If it means one of you needs to put in more hours for a while or go on the road to grow your customer base, offer to be there for the family and do not complain that your spouse isn't home by 6pm for dinner.

Supporting one another and understanding that both of you have an important role will help you get through financially hard times. Also, be cognizant of your expenses. If things are tight and one spouse is now eating and cooking all meals at home to save money but the other spouse is still eating out all the time it can lead to tension and resentment when it is time to pay the bills.

Dialogue: According to Al
Al is a frugal businessman with a positive, realistic outlook. We were discussing debt, investment, and the value of money over time. He put his hand on my shoulder in a fatherly manner and said quietly "Here is the best advice I can give you. Don't spend all your money buying *depreciating* assets."

Appreciating assets increase in value over time. They include (but are not limited to) homes, land, precious stones and metals, antiques, and even classic guitars. Depreciating assets dive. They include (but are not limited to) items such as automobiles, furniture, clothing, appliances, computers, restaurant meals, and vacations.

Al sees important differences between mortgage debt and consumer debt. Mortgage debt buys an inflation-beating, appreciating asset everyone needs. In a financial emergency, the homeowner can usually sell, pay off the loan, and have cash left over.

In contrast, a consumer loan is almost always used to buy depreciating assets people want but do not really need. These items plummet in value the moment they are used. Even if you can sell the asset, you are still on the hook for the balance of the loan.

A mortgage carries other financial advantages as well. Interest on mortgage debt is tax-deductible. Certain home improvements, such as insulation and storm windows, sometimes garner state income tax credits. And if the home or part of it is used as an office, more deductions come into play. Until lawmakers plug these loopholes (and they will someday), these make mortgages a better deal.

Dialogue Starters:
- ➤ What percentage of your annual income is used to purchase appreciating assets?
- ➤ Are the practices of saving and investing contrary to God's Word?
- ➤ What do you expect your children to do with the financial wealth they inherit from you?

Chapter 6 Men and Women

Question 1: **Why can't I remember what it was that brought me to love my wife?**

Question 2: **I am afraid to talk to my husband about things dear to my heart. It seems he does not want to talk about things that matter most to me. How can I do this and get his attention?**

Question 3: **What can you do when your husband won't be the spiritual leader?**

Question 4: **Is it okay to keep something from your spouse? (Nothing major, but a minor thing.)**

Question 5: **How do you stop the tapes of memories from past relationships from entering into your marriage?**

Question 6: **How do you respond when your spouse has promised to deal with a situation one way but then does something else, even though you have reminded him/her?**

Question 7: **How do you deal with an insecure spouse who does not have faith that the Lord will heal and help the marriage?**

Question 8: **How do you know when your expectations for your spouse are too high or unreasonable?**

Question 9: **What do you do when you have just had a fight and your spouse won't tell you what's wrong?**

Question 10: **What do you do when you feel your spouse isn't really listening and you've tried many times to express your feelings?**

Question 11: **What do you do when your husband is unwilling to compromise on even the smallest matter, won't listen to you, believes he is always right, disregards your feelings, and ignores the evidence pointing the other way?**

Question 12: **Why do women not understand how a man thinks?**

Relationship hurdles

Disappointments are part of life. Often, they come in the form of unmet expectations. Nowhere is this more evident than in marriage.

Years ago, a sorority house on a major university campus brought four marriage/family experts from the faculty and community to discuss marriage. About fifty coeds attended the session, billed as "The Truth About Marriage". One of the experts began her presentation by asking a series of questions. "How many of you hope to be married some day? Just raise your hands and keep them up, please." Nearly every young lady in the room raised her hand. "Now, if you know of someone besides your grandparents who enjoy a happy marriage, keep your hand up." After a few awkward moments, almost every hand in the room went down. Two coeds still had hands in the air. The expert commented, "Most of you expect to be married, but you also know from experience that a happy marriage is rare, indeed."

While the expert's approach seemed a bit brutal, she did successfully draw attention to the issue of expectations and the likelihood of disappointment. The questions we field from marriage seminar participants reveal deep disappointments, often around the issues of intimacy and companionship.

These questions and answers illustrate that, despite the disappointments in life, couples can address the issues honestly and, over time, cultivate a sweeter, happier relationship. However, a deeper and more abiding purpose than "happiness" is necessary.

Question 1: Why can't I remember what it was that brought me to love my wife?

This question has a note of sadness. You can and do remember, but you are concentrating solely on your sadness and disappointment. I can only suggest:

> ➢ Be honest. Set aside your pride and say what brought you to love your wife.
> ➢ Be honest. Understand that she is the same person with whom you fell in love.
> ➢ Be honest. Forgive her weaknesses.
> ➢ Be honest. Confess yours.
> ➢ Be honest. Spend the rest of your life rediscovering your love for her.

This may not be a bad thing. People change from life experiences or as they get older. Focus on who you are now as individuals and how that works for you together as partners. Think of this as a new opportunity to date your wife and learn about her just as you did when you first met. Ask her what she thinks about little silly things and what her favorite color is. All the goofy things you would ask someone when you are first getting to know them. Even if you think you know the answers, ask anyway.

Question 2: I am afraid to talk to my husband about things dear to my heart. It seems he does not want to talk about things that matter most to me. How can I do this and get his attention?

You say, "it seems", and that is a great place to start. It seems he is not interested in your thoughts. This may be true. Or, it may be that you think you are sharing your heart while he thinks you are pointing out his inadequacies.

For example, you may worry about having enough money to send the kids to college. You are saying, "I am worried about our finances," but he hears, "It is your fault we don't have enough money." Again, you may be saying "I need you to hold me", while he hears "I don't want to have sex with you!"

Beyond constant patience and forbearance, you may need to get some martial counseling. It is reasonable for you to:

➢ Ask that he listen to you and care about your perspective.
➢ Expect this communication to be free from unfair criticism and blame.

It is possible that your husband is just hearing nagging and complaining. If this is not your intent, try writing a letter. Think of some of the things you would like to discuss. Include the fact that you love him and that it is important for you to share your thoughts with him. Keep it at least 24 hours without reading it. Then look at it again and re-read it to make sure that it is an informative letter and not full of emotional accusations. When you feel that it is a sincere letter, give it to him to read and give him time and space to read it. Let your spouse know that it was not written as an avoidance and that you are there to discuss it. If it is full of emotional accusations then it will not help open dialogue. If this does not help to open dialogue between you, schedule an appointment to meet with a counselor.

Question 3: What can you do when your husband won't be the spiritual leader?

Trying to coerce your husband to lead is impossible. Even if you succeed, you will resent having to do so. To avoid this trap, it is vital that you:

➤ Understand that "spiritual" is not just limited to prayer, church, and personal devotions.
➤ Search for areas in which your husband is providing a godly example (e.g., he works hard, is honest, likes to play with his children, holds his tongue instead of lashing out, does not drink, does not gamble, etc.)
➤ Compliment the positives rather than dwelling only on the negatives.
➤ Build on the compliments by asking him to try his godly leadership in other areas.

Lead by example. Live your life to honor God. Nagging him into it won't work. He has to want to do this. He might be uncomfortable acting as the leader for a variety of reasons. He might think that you know more about it than he does or that he just doesn't know enough to be a leader. He may not put a level of importance on it.

Joining a ladies' bible study could be helpful for you. The other ladies in the bible study might open your eyes to your relationship based on a better understanding of their experiences. We tend to get a vision in our minds that everyone else's situation is perfect and that isn't necessarily the case. You may gain a perspective to help you understand your husband is a leader in the other ways that Jim mentioned above.

Question 4: Is it okay to keep something from your spouse? (Nothing major, but a minor thing.)

A spouse can break trust by committing a grand sin like adultery. He/she can do similar damage by committing smaller sins, such as lying about how much was spent on the new outboard motor or a new outfit.

If it is as minor as you say, telling your spouse should not be a problem. My guess is that you are avoiding conflict by deleting the details. Many couples get into this pattern. "I won't tell my spouse. He/she would just get upset." Often, this is a mutual agreement. "Oh, I just let him/her do whatever. I'm fine, as long as I don't know about it."

Be sure: Your sins will find you out. When they do, you will have two problems—the original act and your reasons for hiding it. Likewise, as much as you want to look the other way, you will have to face facts someday.

Usually, NO, it is not okay to keep something from Should you tell him about a surprise you are planning for him or the gift you are getting him for your anniversary? No. It should be easy to know why you aren't communicating something. Will your spouse be angry with good reason, i.e., your family is in a financial crisis and you just went out and spent $100 on shoes? That would be a valid reason for a spouse to be angry.

Will your spouse be angry because he has a bad temper, perhaps an addiction of some sort and you are fearful of the consequences? For example, you were at the grocery store checking out and you saw your Ex in the checkout line. You both cordially nodded and said hello and goodbye but that was the extent of the interaction. You know that your husband is irrationally jealous of this Ex. You probably shouldn't tell your husband, but it you find yourself consistently withholding the truth for fear of negative consequences, perhaps you should consult a counselor.

There are times in life when an illegitimate demand is made on you. This can be true for a culture or for a relationship. For example, the Nazi party lost its legitimacy when people were asked if they were hiding Jews. If your spouse acts out in violence to you or your children, the legitimacy of your relationship has been lost.. Again, this would be a good time to seek out a counselor.

Having integrity is a two way street. If you are a person with moral integrity, you will know in your gut when you are keeping something from your spouse that is harmful to the marriage.

Question 5 —How do you stop the tapes of memories from past relationships from entering into your marriage?

First of all, it's not just "tapes". It's real consequences. If you or your spouse were sexually involved with others before you married, you have all the normal marital difficulties plus:

➢ Real and imagined memories of intense sexual pleasure (forbidden fruit, often secured with the assistance of drugs and alcohol) which make marital sex seem dull in comparison.
➢ Realistic reasons to mistrust each other.
➢ Temptation to blame the spouse for all marital problems, playing the "tapes" to prove your point.
➢ Sin yet-to-be-confessed and forgiven.
➢ Different sins yield different consequences. However, all sin is similar in that it betrays the human inability to keep God's Law. Your sins are nailed to the cross of Christ, as are mine. Leave them there and enjoy a clean, wholesome life. Go, and sin no more!

When any sort of unhealthy or negative thought starts to enter your mind, if it is unproductive, try to focus on something else. Count out loud, think about your kids and something fun you did as a family on your last vacation. Phone a friend you know will distract you to a different subject and thought. You can choose to think these things or recognize that the thoughts are creeping into your head and push them out with other thoughts. It is possible to retrain your brain and thoughts to be generally more uplifting and positive, but you must be consistent.

Whenever any negative or unpleasant thought enters the mind, very quickly change the thought even if it means thinking nothing at all. If a song triggers a memory, change the station or turn off the radio. If it is a place, avoid it. Eventually you will have retrained your thought where you don't have to do this anymore.

Question 6 —How do you respond when your spouse has promised to deal with a situation one way but then does something else, even though you have reminded him/her?

Without more details, I am in the dark. However, let me try to find a light switch!

Some spouses make promises not because they really intend to keep them, but to placate the other spouse and avoid confrontation. For example, a husband may promise to fix a broken shutter to get his wife to stop complaining about it. She becomes angrier as each rotted, broken slat breaks off and falls into the bushes. Every time she reminds him, he says, "Sure, I'll do that," but does not follow-through. To her, it is not a broken shutter. It is a broken marital promise. Likewise, a wife may promise to go away for a weekend with her husband, yet forget and book a church meeting for that time.

The same thing can happen in other situations. For example, a husband might get his wife to promise that she will not criticize him in front of the children. When she forgets and does so, he feels crushed. Likewise, a wife might get her husband to promise he will not get into a theological argument in Sunday school class. When he does, she feels humiliated and betrayed. Stop making promises you are not committed to keep. Start by taking some sound advice:

➤ Don't make promises on the spur of the moment. If you are on the phone and your spouse asks you to fix something, don't blankly nod "yes". Instead, say, "Let's talk about that after I am off the phone."

➤ Discipline yourself to sit down and share your misgivings. "I want to make your favorite meal

124

this week, but honestly, I don't think I can get home in time."

> Share your problem with some close friends. Ask them to hold you accountable. (You probably will fix the shutter as promised if you know this is first on your small group prayer list for next week!)

The answer above is fine. However, be careful that you don't develop a passive aggressive manner in dealing with each other. Just say no in the first place instead of saying something and then not following through.

Question 7—How do you deal with an insecure spouse who does not have faith that the Lord will heal and help the marriage?

Here are some tips for dealing with a spouse who is wavering in his/her faith:

➢ Remember that you cannot make someone else have faith.
➢ Face honestly your own misbehavior. When it is true, admit, "I know that a lot of your insecurity comes from me not giving you the love you need. Forgive me and be patient with me."
➢ Confess your own struggles with faith.
➢ Remember, trust is always a two-way street. You may pride yourself on being the faithful one while casting your mate as the one with all the trust problems. In reality, you both may have serious doubts that could be addressed.

I don't believe the Lord alone can heal a marriage. I believe that by refocusing your life and your decisions based on the way God would want you to live your life, you can rebuild your marriage. At the end of the day, it is still up to the two of you to work at healing the marriage through honesty and integrity.

Question 8—How do you know when your expectations for your spouse are too high or unreasonable?

This is best tested in consultation with solid Christian friends, pastors, teachers, and counselors. You know your expectations are unreasonable when:

> - You are concerned primarily with personal happiness.
> - You insist that long-standing character traits be changed overnight.
> - You usually say "If you really love me, you will . . ."
> - Jesus Himself would disappoint you.

Unreasonable expectations are a problem, but so are non-existent expectations. Asking your spouse to be faithful, sober, honest, and hard-working is not asking too much. If you are tolerating alcoholism, irresponsibility, sloth, or infidelity, raise your expectations!

Are your expectations something you could live up to? Are these new expectations since you married? For example, if, when you were dating, your spouse always had stacks of papers on his desk, you can't expect that now that you are married he will not have those same stacks. Are you trying to remake this individual into your own image rather than who they are?

Question 9 —What do you do when you have just had a fight and your spouse won't tell you what's wrong?

I take it that you found yourself arguing about a trivial matter but feeling that there is more to the problem. If this is true:

➢ Say so. For example, "You seem to be upset about more than just the kids spilling juice on the carpet. What's wrong?"
➢ Invite further communication. For example, "When you are ready to talk, I'll be ready to listen."
➢ Be honest about your fears. For example, "When you clam up like this, I start imagining all the things that might be wrong. You could have cancer, or be having an affair, or be thinking about quitting your job. I would worry less if you would just tell me."
➢ Understand that your spouse's silence may be the result of your past unwillingness to listen. If you have jumped him/her for speaking honestly in the past, confess this. For example, "I know that in the past I have asked you to communicate and then screamed at you when you tried. Forgive me and give me another chance."

Give the person some time to calm down. Then with a calm tone and sincerity, let your spouse know that you really care about what is bothering him or her. You want to listen. The key here is that if they start talking, you need to shut up and listen.

Question 10—What do you do when you feel your spouse isn't really listening and you've tried many times to express your feelings?

The word "listening" implies congruent action. When a person listens, he/she responds in some appropriate, consistent, observable way. For example, a wife might say, "I am afraid we cannot afford a new car." If her husband says, "I understand" but continues shopping for a new car, she gets the sense that he is not listening.

The clearest communication is characterized by congruent context, words, tone of voice, action, tentative interpretations, and (most importantly!) the serious consideration of alternatives. If your spouse is not listening, consider the possibility that you are sending mixed signals and inviting the same in return.

Question 11—What do you do when your husband is unwilling to compromise on even the smallest matter, won't listen to you, believes he is always right, disregards your feelings, and ignores the evidence pointing the other way?

Taken at face value, I would say you married a stupid, thoughtless mule. However, I am certain that a sharp lady would not fall for such a beast! While your husband is probably stubborn and insensitive, you may be addressing these faults in a manner that makes matters worse.

I have seen many marriage counseling sessions begin this way. One-spouse states accusations as a simple matter of fact, while the other spouse gets defensive and counter-attacks with accusations of his/her own. Unless something is done to change this sequence, every meeting will degenerate into a competition to see which one can win the therapist's favor by best vilifying the other.

To break the cycle, it is vital that one spouse (usually the one with the strongest faith and self-efficacy) gives up the strategic high ground and risks being vulnerable. For example, you might:

➢ Recall the strengths that first attracted you to your husband. Usually, these are the same qualities that have come to irritate you.

➢ Remind your husband that you married him for those strengths, e.g., "Honey, I fell in love with your strong will and ability to keep going no matter what."

➢ Confess your weakness, e.g., "I know I am often critical of the decisions you make. Sometimes it is because I really do know a better way, but sometimes it is because I am mule-headed, too."

➢ Ask for love, e.g., "When I am tired, weak, or frightened, I need you to be patient with me, to listen to me, and to assure me you love me and will stay beside me."

Question 12— Why do women not understand how a man thinks?

In a culture that idolizes education, I am tempted to say "from lack of information." However, I know many men and women who prefer fantasy to fact.

"Why?" can be a bad question when it leads away from honest self-examination. A better way to ask this might be "What prevents my wife from understanding how I think?" or "What prevents me from communicating how I think?" If this is really what you want to know, consider the following possible answers:

➢ Your wife probably does not understand you because you clam-up and/or get defensive when she wants to discuss something.

➢ Your wife may be uncomfortable with the responsibility that "knowing" brings. Often times people play dumb because they know that the minute they affirm that the other person has a point they become responsible for doing something about it.

➢ You may be communicating that your wife is to blame for the majority of your marital difficulties. No one enjoys being told, under the guise of intimate communication, that she is a failure.

Because we are women. Seriously, our brains process information in a different way than men. I know society tells us all that we are equal but in fact, this is NOT true. This doesn't mean we are inferior to men, it just means we are different. That is a good thing!

Chapter 7: Questions Therapists Dream Will Be Asked (But Often Aren't!)

Question 1: **I am a selfish, thoughtless husband. I need to get my mind off my desires and on what is best for my wife and children. Where in the Bible can I find the instruction I need?**

Question 2: **When I'm angry at my husband, I simply refuse to have sex with him for several months. I need his forgiveness and his love. What can I do to restore our relationship?**

Question 3: **I drink a lot and blame it on my spouse and kids. I need to get sober and spend the rest of my life on the wagon. What is the best way to begin?**

Question 4: **I depend on my mother and father, not my spouse, to meet my financial and emotional needs. I need to develop a closer, more intimate relationship with my spouse. How can I put some financial and emotional distance between my parents and myself?**

Question 5: **I often sit passively and criticize while my wife provides the religious guidance in our family. I need to learn to be a real servant leader. Can you recommend someone who would spend an hour a week with me to teach me the skills I need?**

Question 6: **My spouse and I have an appointment with a marriage counselor. How can we avoid wasting time and get the maximum value for our counseling dollar?**

Question 7: **Who can I tell about my counseling session?**

Dream Questions

Skeptics may suspect we have loaded the previous sections with our own softball questions and easy answers. They are wrong. With the exception of correcting a few spelling errors and some minor editing of grammar, the questions are verbatim. We have, however, developed a list of Dream Questions—seldom-asked queries we wish more people would ask—and the answers we would love to give.

Dream Question 1: I am a selfish, thoughtless husband. I need to get my mind off my desires and on what is best for my wife and children. Where in the Bible can I find the instruction I need?

> Begin with the 5th chapter of Ephesians, verses 21-33. Take the key words you find there (e.g., reverence, submission, love, splendor, respect, etc.) and use a concordance to study each of these concepts. If you do not have a concordance, buy one at your local Christian bookstore.
> If necessary, ask your pastor to help you. He would be tickled to assist you in finding Scriptural answers to this marvelous question.

As we have mentioned before, the 12 steps are principles borrowed from various places in the Bible. If followed they can be very helpful.

Dream Question 2: When I'm angry at my husband, I simply refuse to have sex with him for several months. I need his forgiveness and his love. What can I do to restore our relationship?

You are well on your way already. Don't just hop in bed and pretend everything is OK. If serious moral or ethical matters separate you and your husband, seek Christian marriage counseling immediately. If your anger is built around trivial and imagined wrongs,

> ➢ Confess this to him and ask him to forgive you.
> ➢ Kiss him and tell him that you need him.
> ➢ Use your Bible and concordance to study the word "anger".
> ➢ Ask a Christian female friend to meet regularly with you for prayer and accountability.
> ➢ Look forward to great days and nights ahead!

You both need to address this issue from a holistic approach. Something else is likely going on that made you angry in the first place. You both may have some unhealthy patterns, which you have fallen into, and the only way you now know to respond is to withhold sex. If everything else was great in your relationship you most likely wouldn't have an issue with sex. Start by asking your spouse to sit with you and talk in a neutral place like your living room, not the bedroom. Calmly bring the subject up and express concern for the place your relationship currently resides. If you are afraid of being rejected then it may help you to speak with a counselor.

Instead of starting out by TALKING, start out by asking your spouse how he feels about your

137

relationship. Then as hard as it may be, LISTEN to your spouse without interrupting even if you are getting angry or offended. Just listen. Try not to respond defensively. Try to summarize what you think your spouse just said to you about the relationship. For example, " What I hear you saying is that you feel our relationship is now lacking the spark and communication that we once had. Do you agree that is what you are saying?"

Then again, LISTEN.

Hearing your summary of the state of the relationship may help your spouse open up give you a starting point to work from on rebuilding communication.

You may need to go together to a counselor for a few sessions to help you get on the right track.

Dream Question 3: I drink a lot and blame it on my spouse and kids. I need to get sober and spend the rest of my life on the wagon. What is the best way to begin?

It is best to consider alcohol THE problem. Unless it is removed from the equation, nothing will ever add up. I recommend that you:

> Seek medical treatment immediately.
> Begin attending a Twelve Step program. It will help to have others around you who really know what it is like to get and stay sober.

First, accept that you are the only one that makes you do anything and second, be glad that you recognize this is an issue. This means there is HOPE for you to have the kind of life you will be proud of. Find a few AA meetings to attend. Then find a sponsor and work the 12 steps for the rest of your life. Disassociate yourself from your "drinking friends". Associate yourself with people you respect, who have moral integrity, and who are friends of your marriage and your family.

Dream Question 4: I depend on my mother and father, not my spouse, to meet my financial and emotional needs. I need to develop a closer, more intimate relationship with my spouse. How can I put some financial and emotional distance between my parents and myself?

Such a question would reflect great insight, sorrow, and repentance. Moreover, it would represent a wonderful turn to honesty and sincerity. For those who might ask such a question, I recommend:

➢ Confess your sin to your spouse.
➢ See a Christian family therapist to work out a strategy for establishing firm yet flexible boundaries.
➢ Don't tell your parents you are getting this help, don't ask them to pay for it, and don't ask them to take care of your kids while you go.
➢ Understand that your parents are as dependent on this relationship as you are, and will be upset when you begin to pull away.
➢ Decide that you will obey God's command to "leave and cleave" no matter what your parents say.

If you are old enough to have a spouse, you should not be relying on your relatives for financial and emotional needs. Now there is a caveat: Our emotional needs are fulfilled by relationships in our lives, which can include parents. But this should not be your primary source.

As for finances , you and your spouse should sit down and make a list of your necessary living expenses, or needs, and then a list of your 'wants'.

Write down how much you have together to cover those expenses. If you don't have enough, start cutting from the 'want' category Perhaps one of you may need to consider a career change or a part time job in order to eliminate debt. If necessary, seek the help of a financial counselor. Then stop taking money from your parents. If possible, start paying them back for some of the money they have given you over the years.

Dream Question 5: *I often sit passively and criticize while my wife provides the religious guidance in our family. I need to learn to be a real servant leader. Can you recommend someone who would spend an hour a week with me to teach me the skills I need?*

The best way to begin is by calling your pastor or minister and asking, "Will you teach me the principles of spiritual leadership?" This will be hard for you, since you have probably sat passively in church and criticized your preacher as he/she tried to teach you these things. Set aside time to study and pray with a godly leader. Don't just charge in and take command. Instead, be patient with your wife as you learn to express (and she learns to accept) your godly leadership.

Look for a men's small group in your community or church. Reach out to your pastor for a recommendation on who you connect with as well as for reading materials that might be useful.

D

ialogue: Help for Mike and Mary

A light snow was beginning to stick to the driveway. Mike pressed the button activating the automatic garage door, drove in, and shut off the car engine. Resting his head for a moment on the steering wheel, he remembered the e-mail message he had received that morning. "I just can't tell her," he thought.

As he hung his fleece parka in the hall closet, Mike glanced at the little decorative mirror mounted on the wall just to his left. In its reflection, he could see the sparkling lights of the Christmas tree and the dozens of green, red, and gold wrapped packages resting under its boughs. Though he knew he would feel a twinge of guilt for it, he cursed quietly.

The boss had been brutal. "Beginning January 2, all sales associates will report directly to me. Managers who want to stay on-board can apply for one of the two new associate jobs. These are commission only, so I imagine most of you will be looking elsewhere. You'll each get two weeks' pay and your Christmas gift."

"Fifteen years, and I get an e-mail, two week's pay, and a cheese log," Mike hissed. Alone in the darkened hallway, he sensed that his bitterness was really fear. Can I make it on commission only? What if I can't find another job here? What if we have to move? What about Mary's job? He had never wanted his children to bounce from school to school the way he had, always alone. Always alone. He felt his steel blue eyes beginning to mist. Breathing deeply, he rubbed his eyes, regained control, and lied to himself, "Must be catching a cold."

Mike shuffled into the kitchen. The recently remodeled galley, with its custom white cabinets, lemon-yellow counters, and red and blue gingham checked café curtains, was brightly lit but empty. The muffled sound of the dryer told him Mary was downstairs doing laundry. Trying to sound light-hearted, he began rummaging through the refrigerator and yelled, "Hey, is any of that roast left from last night?"

Mary heard him, but did not answer. Struggling up the wooden stairs with a large plastic laundry basket, she stumbled in and dramatically dumped a pile of clean underwear in the middle of the white vinyl floor. This effectively trapped her husband, who was standing over the sink finishing his sandwich.

Mary's eyes moved quickly from Mike's face to the sandwich and back. "The dinner the kids fixed for you is in there. Be sure to thank them before you flip on the ball game as usual. And . . . ," she snapped, turning away and heading back down the stairs," Your old buddy Bob left a little message on the answering machine. I didn't know you were planning to go golfing again this weekend."

Dialogue Starters:
➢ How does the context (late evening, frustrated parents, demanding kids, and Bob's phone call) affect their communication?
➢ What is Mike trying to accomplish by keeping the news from Mary?
➢ What did he actually communicate?
➢ What is Mary trying to say with her words and actions?

144

Dream Question 6: My spouse and I have an appointment with a marriage counselor. How can we avoid wasting time and get the maximum value for our counseling dollar?

Should you find yourself stuck and in need of professional therapy, you can make the most of your counseling time in the following manner:

> ➤ Pray that God will speak through your counselor. Remember that he/she is an ambassador for Jesus Christ, responsible for helping you apply His Word to your life. Hunger and thirst for righteousness, and you will be filled.
> ➤ Write down questions and bring them to the session. Give them to your counselor at the beginning of the hour. Most of the hour can then be spent identifying workable problems, exploring possible solutions, and planning appropriate action.
> ➤ Arrive a few minutes early. Use these minutes to check in, fill-out registration materials, and pray. Arriving late ensures a hurried, less-than-productive counseling hour.
> ➤ Tell your counselor what you hope to get out of the counseling session. Even if you have been seen before, your counselor does not know what motivated you to make this appointment nor what you expect from it. Be straightforward about your expectations.
> ➤ Maximize first-person narrative (e.g., "I did . . .", "We want . . .", etc.). Take personal responsibility for your part in the problem and

- plan to make changes in your thoughts and behavior. You should confess your sins, seek forgiveness, and plan to make restitution.
- Minimize third-person narrative (e.g., "He said . . .", "They went . . .", etc.) If you spend the entire hour recounting past events and the actions of others, you will miss valuable opportunities to examine yourself and plan appropriate changes.
- Consider including a family member or friend in the counseling sessions. Many personal problems are caused or made worse by relationship problems. God expects family and friends - not professionals - to provide the long-term love, support, and confrontation needed for a healthy life. The people closest to you will either be part of the problem or part of the solution.
- Be aware of the time. As the hour comes to a close, allow your counselor to summarize, make recommendations, and pray. Consider the thoughts and feelings of the next person who is waiting to see the counselor.
- Pay your fee. It has cost your counselor many years and about $100,000 to prepare to provide this assistance for you and your loved ones. If he/she has not charged a fee, send the church a love offering designated "counseling ministry".
- Practice confidentiality (exceptions include your spouse or, if you are a minor, your parents.) You trust the counselor to keep quiet about your counseling session. He/she should be able to trust you to do so as well.

BE HONEST! LISTEN with an open mind and heart.

146

Dream Question 7: Who can I tell about my counseling session?

Of course, you can tell anyone you want. In sharp contrast, your counselor cannot tell anyone anything about the session. He/she is bound by law to respect and keep confidentiality, with a few exceptions: For example, if you confess a crime or give the counselor reason to believe you are committing or will commit a crime (e.g. child abuse, murder, etc.), or if you threaten to harm yourself or someone else, the counselor is bound by law to report this to the appropriate local law enforcement agency.

If you decide to share the content of your counseling sessions with others, consider the following guidelines.

> ➤ Be honestly excited about insights gained. Keep the focus on positive personal achievements, not all the details of your presenting problem.

> ➤ If you are honestly disturbed about what you believe the counselor said, talk with him/her directly. Then get a second opinion from another counselor.

> ➤ Don't blame your problems on others, or manipulate friends and family to sympathize with you by telling them about your counseling sessions. Over the long haul, this approach will force people away from you.

This really depends. Why are you telling others? If you are telling them just to vent and bash your spouse then it may not be so great to talk about it. If you are talking about it because it is helping you and you want to help someone else by sharing how you are growing and developing etc. then this is a different story.

Notice that each dream question begins with an honest self-judgment, reflects an accurate assessment of personal need, and implies a concrete commitment to godly action. None puts the presenter on the spot. Each elicits a straight-forward, practical response.

Even if you never attend a dynamite marriage enrichment retreat, God will give you many opportunities to develop and ask such questions. Your minister may preach a sermon which sets you thinking. A Christian radio program might stir your soul. A friend might confront you with an obvious inconsistency in your life. Your spouse may ask you to read a book or article which discusses a concern he/she has. Your specific issues might be very different, but the formula for a good question is the same: Absolute honesty, accurate assessment of need, and concrete commitment to godly action.

As Jesus said, "You have not because you ask not." He also said "Ask and you will receive; seek, and you will find; knock, and the door will be opened to you." Good questions are the secret to a good life!

Let us conclude with the following Exercise:

Exercise: The Personals Ad

Take a step back from your marriage. Look at your spouse as an individual. Were you to die, your spouse would be available to date. Write a personal ad to highlight why someone else would be lucky to date this person.

www.ingramcontent.com/pod-product-compliance
Lightning Source LLC
Chambersburg PA
CBHW07075729O326
41931CB00011BA/2054